THE REMINISCENCES OF
Rear Admiral Harold J. Bernsen
U.S. Navy (Retired)

INTERVIEWED BY
Paul Stillwell

U.S. Naval Institute • Annapolis, Maryland

Copyright © 2014

Preface

This oral history grew out of a series of interviews I did in January 1988 while serving on active duty as a Naval Reservist. Artist William Phillips and I traveled together to the Persian Gulf/Gulf of Oman area on behalf of the Naval Historical Center. He collected images, and I collected the words of individuals serving in Operation Earnest Will, the U.S. Navy escort of Kuwaiti oil tankers that had been registered under the U.S. flag. Bill turned his experiences and observations into a series of paintings. In the course of our three weeks in the area, I completed 75 taped interviews, with the subjects spanning the range from flag officers to a ship's cook and a Marine sentry. Those interviews provided on-the-spot descriptions of the varied ways in which the Navy, Marine Corps, and Coast Guard worked to keep the flow of oil going between Kuwait at the northern end of the Persian Gulf and the Strait of Hormuz that marked its southern entrance and exit.

Of the 75 interviews, the tapes came out fine on all but one—Admiral Bernsen's. To rectify that problem he subsequently agreed to additional interviews for the Naval Institute. The disadvantage of that approach is that the events were not as fresh in his mind as they were at the time Operation Earnest Will was in progress. The advantages were that he was able to gain perspective from subsequent events, and he was able to be more candid after retiring from active duty than he had been while still in service. Admiral Bernsen subsequently did interviews for three books that related to his Persian Gulf service:

Harold Lee Wise, *Inside the Danger Zone: the U.S. Military in the Persian Gulf, 1987-1988* (Annapolis: Naval Institute Press, 2007).

Lee Allen Zatarain, *Tanker War: America's First Conflict with Iran, 1987-1988* (Philadelphia: Casemate, 2008).

David Crist, *The Twilight War: the Secret History of America's Thirty-Year Conflict with Iran* (New York: Penguin Press, 2012).

The admiral's recollections appear piecemeal in the three books above. One benefit of the oral history is that Admiral Bernsen's descriptions of that tour of duty are here gathered in one place. A second benefit is that the oral history deals with topics not covered in the three books. In dealing with the original raw transcripts of the interviews, I did an initial round of editing for the sake of accuracy, clarity, and smoothness. In addition, I inserted footnotes for the benefit of readers and posed further questions to the admiral. He responded to the queries and did some further editing of his own. The final version has his blessing.

Thanks go to Ms. Janis Jorgensen of the Naval Institute staff who has coordinated the printing and binding of the finished product. In completing this volume, the Naval Institute expresses its gratitude to the Tawani Foundation and the Pritzker Military Library of Chicago for their generous financial support of the oral history program that produced this memoir.

Paul Stillwell
U.S. Naval Institute
December 2014

REAR ADMIRAL HAROLD JOHN BERNSEN
UNITED STATES NAVY (RETIRED)

Harold John Bernsen was born in Boston on 25 November 1936, the son of Harold and Solveig Bernsen. After completing his studies at Boston's Roxbury Latin School, he participated in the regular Naval Reserve Officer Training Corps program while a student at Dartmouth College in Hanover, New Hampshire. Upon his graduation in June 1958, he was commissioned an ensign and reported to flight training. Designated a naval aviator in March 1960, he received orders to Carrier Airborne Early Warning Squadron 12 at Quonset Point, Rhode Island. While attached to VAW-12 Bernsen served with detachments operating E-1B Tracers on various East Coast aircraft carriers.

From October 1963 to October 1966, Bernsen was attached to the Defense Intelligence Agency in Washington, D.C. He was next ordered to duty as aide and flag lieutenant on the staff of Commander Carrier Division Seven in the Pacific. He was promoted to lieutenant commander in January 1967.

He reported to Carrier Airborne Early Warning Squadron 120 (RVAW-120) in Norfolk, Virginia, in October 1968 for familiarization training in the E-2B Hawkeye aircraft. He subsequently completed two Mediterranean deployments with VAW-126 on board the USS *Forrestal* (CVA-59). Following a tour under instruction at the Armed Forces Staff College, Norfolk, Virginia, during which he was promoted to commander, he returned to VAW-126 in February 1972 to become executive officer and subsequently commanding officer of the squadron. He reported to the *Forrestal* in April 1974 as navigator, completing his fourth and fifth successive deployments on board CVA-59.

From December 1975 to April 1977 he commanded RVAW-120, the training squadron for the E-2 aircraft. Following this command tour, he served for two years in the office of the Deputy Chief of Naval Operations for Air Warfare (OP-05) in Washington, D.C., the first year as the E-2 aircraft program coordinator, the second as head of the program management section. On 1 July 1979 he was promoted to captain.

Having assumed command of the USS *La Salle* (AGF-3), the flagship of Commander Middle East Force, in March 1980, he served with her in the Persian Gulf during the hostage crisis in Iran and the initiation of the Iran/Iraq War. From March 1982 until the spring of 1983, Bernsen was assigned as executive assistant to the chief of staff of the Supreme Allied Commander Atlantic in Norfolk, Virginia. In June 1983 he assumed command of the Navy's training carrier, the USS *Lexington* (AVT-16). Relieved in December 1984, Bernsen was promoted to rear admiral and assumed duties as Director of Plans, Policy and Programs for the United States Central Command in March 1985. He assumed duties as Commander Middle East Force on 5 July 1986 and served in that billet until February 1988.

Bernsen was promoted to rear admiral (upper half—two stars) in 1988 while serving as N-5, Director of Plans and Policy, on the staff of Commander in Chief Atlantic Fleet in Norfolk, Virginia. He completed his 33½-year naval career as Deputy and Chief of Staff, CinCLantFlt, retiring 1 December 1991.

Admiral Bernsen's military decorations include the Distinguished Service Medal with gold star; Defense Superior Service Medal; Legion of Merit; Defense Meritorious Service Medal with gold star; Meritorious Service Medal; Joint Services Commendation Medal; Navy Commendation Medal; Navy Achievement Medal; Bahrain Order First Class; Royal Norwegian Order of Merit; and various theater and campaign awards.

After leaving active service, Bernsen served as a consultant to various defense-related research and analysis organizations and private industry, principally with regard to defense and security issues in the Middle East. In 1995 Bernsen formed his own company, Overseas Environmental Marketing, Inc., for the purpose of forming joint ventures in the Arabian Gulf region to process oily waste water and refine waste oil.

From January 1998 to August 2001 he served as chairman and then president of 21st Century Coatings, Inc., a domestic manufacturer of industrial coatings. In late 2001 he sold his interest in the company and retired from active business management.

From 2002 through 2004 he participated as a consultant and pre-incorporation director of the UNICORN Group, contributing to the successful establishment of an Islamic investment bank headquartered in Bahrain.

From 2010 through 2012 he served as Director of Middle East Operations for Advanced BioCatalytics Corporation of Irvine, California, a manufacturer of environmentally friendly petroleum-related cleaning products.

He has donated considerable time and energy to the non-profit world as chairman/director of seven quite diverse organizations noted below.

Listed in *Marquis Who's Who in America* since 1991.

Boards:

    Director, Hampton Roads World Affairs Council, since 2009

    Director American Bahraini Friendship Society (Washington-based non-profit dedicated to improving relations between the United States and Bahrain), since 1992

    President of the Board, Norwegian Lady Foundation (Norfolk-based non-profit committed to the preservation of the Norwegian Lady state and plaza site at the Virginia Beach oceanfront), since 2003

    Director, Hawkeye Association (Norfolk-based naval aviation-related organization), since 1991

    Director Emeritus, Past Chairman of the Board, 1999-2007, National Council on U.S.-Arab Relations (Washington-based non-profit devoted to improving Arab-American understanding)

    Trustee, formerly President of the Trustees from 2000 to 2005, Physicians for Peace (non-profit headquartered in Norfolk, Virginia, providing international health care service to those in need in the developing world

    Director Emeritus, National U.S.-Arab Chamber of Commerce, Washington, D.C.

Admiral Bernsen was married to the former Doris Champion of Shelby, North Carolina, until her death in 2013. His stepson is Stephen Jolly, PhD.

Deed of Gift

The U.S. Naval Institute is hereby authorized to make available to individuals, libraries, and other repositories of its choosing the tapes and/or transcripts of ten oral history interviews concerning the life and naval career of the undersigned. The Naval Institute may also, at its discretion, use the material in electronic/digital format, including posting on the Internet. The interviews were recorded on 18 November 1991 and 12 September 1997 in collaboration with Paul Stillwell for the U.S. Naval Institute.

The undersigned does hereby release and assign to the U.S. Naval Institute the rights and title to these interviews, with the exception that the undersigned retains the right to use the material for his own purposes, as he sees fit. The copyright in both the oral and transcribed versions shall be the property of the U.S. Naval Institute. The tape recordings of the interviews are and will remain the property of the U.S. Naval Institute.

Signed and sealed this 4th day of December 2014.

Harold J. Bernsen
Rear Admiral, U.S. Navy (Retired)

Interview Number 1 with Rear Admiral Harold J. Bernsen, U.S. Navy (Retired)

Place: Center for Naval Analyses, Arlington, Virginia

Date: Monday, 18 November 1991

Paul Stillwell: Perhaps to begin at the beginning, Admiral, when did you report as Commander Middle East Force, and what essentially was the status quo at that point?

Admiral Bernsen: I reported in June of 1986. I relieved John Addams as Commander Middle East Force.* The situation in the Gulf in June of 1986 was tense. The Iran-Iraq War was in full bloom. There had been a number of attacks by the Iraqis, as well as the Iranians, on the land front.

Between the period of '80 to '85, there was relatively little activity at sea, as I recall. But that began to change as the Iraqis sensed that one way to put pressure on the Iranians was if they could curtail the flow of oil out of Iran onto the world market. Almost all of the Iranian export capacity was funneled through Kharg Island—not all of it but almost all of it—in the northern part of the Gulf, just to the east of the Shatt al-Arab.† So the Iraqis began to concentrate on interrupting the flow of shipping that carried that oil from Kharg Island down the Gulf and out through the Strait of Hormuz to other world ports. They did this by attacking Iranian and other world shipping that was carrying Iranian crude. They did it primarily by attacking those ships in the so-called Iranian self-proclaimed war zone, extending to the south from the coast of Iran and encompassing almost half of the Persian Gulf.

In retaliation for those attacks, the Iranians in turn had decided to attack ships also. But since the Iraqis did not have any ships in the Gulf, in the vicinity of the Gulf, the Strait of Hormuz, or in the Gulf of Oman, the only targets that the Iranians could strike were those which consisted of ships transiting the Gulf and the strait, in trade with

---

* Rear Admiral John F. Addams, USN, was Commander Middle East Force from July 1983 to June 1986.
† Shatt al-Arab (Stream of the Arabs) is a 120-mile-long river that flows from the confluence of the Tigris and Euphrates rivers in Iraq and thence into the Persian Gulf. The southern end is the border between Iran and Iraq.

the Gulf Arabs, all of whom by definition were allies or at least in one way or another in support of the Iraqis.

So you had in essence two quite different anti-shipping regimes, but regardless of the basic difference in the two, the overall result was the same: a Gulf that was confused, frightened, a war zone. There was not a great deal loss of life, but an awful lot of economic destruction, and a really confused and a rather perilous area, particularly if you were a commercial shipper.

Paul Stillwell: One thing we talked about before was your background that led to your selection for that billet.

Admiral Bernsen: Well, my original contact with the Gulf in the Middle East came from a tour I had as the commanding officer of the *La Salle*, which was the flagship for Middle East Force.* That was an unaccompanied tour in the Gulf area from March of 1980 until I left the Gulf at the beginning of December of that same year, although I had the ship for some 13 or 14 months thereafter.†

Then the second tour, the second time I had anything to do with it, was from February-March of '85 until June of '86, when I was the director of plans and policy at CentCom in Tampa.‡ CinCCent, of course, was the unified commander responsible for the Middle East.

That J-5 job was particularly valuable because in that capacity I traveled with the CinC.§ When I first arrived, that was General Bob Kingston, the Army four-star. Then he was relieved in late '85 by George Crist, the Marine commander.** Crist was the commander of our unified forces throughout the Iran-Iraq War period.

So I'd had a fair amount of contact with government officials, military and

---

* USS *La Salle* (LPD-3) was originally commissioned 22 February 1964 as an amphibious transport dock. She served as an amphibious warfare ship until 1 July 1972, when her designation was changed to AGF-3, a miscellaneous flagship. She was flagship of the Middle East Force 1972 to 1980 and 1983 to 1994. She subsequently became flagship for Commander Sixth Fleet.
† Bernsen's command tour in the *La Salle* was from 24 March 1980 to 12 February 1982.
‡ CentCom – U.S. Central Command.
§ J-5 is the designation for the plans section of a joint-service staff.
** General Robert C. Kingston, USA, served as Commander in Chief Central Command from its founding on 1 January 1983 to 27 November 1985. General George B. Crist, USMC, was CinCCent from 27 November 1985 to 23 November 1988.

political, from Egypt to Pakistan. Also, specifically I made many, many trips to the Gulf itself and visited all of the GCC countries at least once or twice before coming over as Middle East Force.[*]

Paul Stillwell: What comparisons might you draw between the status of the staff and the Middle East Force in total from those earlier times, and what you found in 1986?

Admiral Bernsen: Well, basically, there wasn't a huge difference. The staff, quite frankly, was about the same size. I think there were a couple of additional intelligence folks and a couple of radiomen, but in essence the staff was about the same size; the positions were about the same. There really had not been any particular recognition on the part of the Navy's personnel bureaucracy that there was any need to have a larger staff. Later the issue of size became considerably more contentious, as a matter of fact, as the crisis in the area expanded and as the number of ships under my command increased. And they increased dramatically, particularly in 1987.

Paul Stillwell: Well, my perception from visiting the *La Salle* in early '88 was that the staff had grown considerably in a short time.

Admiral Bernsen: Well, that's right. Originally, in the early '80s, the Middle East Force normally consisted of the flagship and two or three small combatants. And they were not necessarily tied to the Persian Gulf. They cruised the area from Mombasa north and into the Red Sea, and certainly over into the North Arabian Sea and Pakistan.

In fact, very often the flagship and one of the other ships would meet and then not see each other again for two or three months at a time. The situation in '86 had changed quite dramatically. There was still a certain amount of movement by the flagship out of the Gulf down to places like Mombasa and so forth. But there was much more of a concentrated emphasis and attention on the Gulf itself, naturally because of the beginnings of the tanker war. More ships were assigned to Middle East Force. If I recall

---

[*] GCC – Gulf Cooperation Council.

correctly, by the time I got there in June of '86, we had *La Salle*, plus, I think, five ships, as part of the force.

The principal function of our force in June of '86 was to maintain a presence, which was particularly valuable from a political standpoint. For example, Bahrain, which had a very, very small navy and very small military, relied very heavily on U.S. political, military, and moral support. The Iranians weren't all that far away. Since Bahrain supported Iraq, tacitly, if not overtly, there certainly would have been opportunity for the Iranians to put considerable pressure on the Bahraini. They felt relatively secure by dint of the fact that the U.S. fleet not only steamed nearby, but, in fact, was semi-home-ported in Bahrain, and ships came and went all the time.

I'm convinced that this made a great deal of difference to the Emir and his government. It made a great deal of difference as to how he acted in his capacity as a sovereign, while countries such as Qatar and the UAE, I think, were less convinced of the actual deterrent value of having a Navy force there.[*] I think that there were certainly some individuals high up in the government in those countries, who did, in fact, recognize that we represented the stabilizing force—a deterrent force—and really sort of a defensive curtain, if you will, that ran right down the Gulf, simply because of the fact that we had a reasonable number of ships moving up and down.

Paul Stillwell: Do you remember some point at which the flagship stopped going outside of the Persian Gulf because the situation demanded your presence?

Admiral Bernsen: I honestly don't remember.

Paul Stillwell: Were you still doing some of that traveling around during the early part of your tour?

Admiral Bernsen: Oh, yes. Maybe the first nine to ten months in my tour, I traveled extensively. For example, the flagship visited Muscat, Oman, steamed all the way around into the Red Sea and visited Djibouti. And we were on our way up the Red Sea

---

[*] UAE – United Arab Emirates.

for a visit to Jeddah, and another visit to Hurghada in Egypt, which would have been the first visit to Hurghada by a U.S. ship in God knows how long.

Just after the Djibouti visit, we had a situation develop in the northern Gulf that was somewhat distressing. I don't remember exactly all the details, but it was sufficiently unnerving to General Crist that he ordered me to get off the flagship, fly over to the Gulf, go on board the USS *O'Bannon* as a temporary flagship, steam up the northern Gulf, while the *La Salle*, at best speed, came around and reentered the Gulf. I think that was in the February-March '87 time frame. So up until that time *La Salle* was still performing, and the staff was still doing, relatively routine things. That included steaming all the way to Djibouti, which was a pretty good steam, as a matter of fact—couple of thousand miles from Bahrain. So that was a pretty good trip.

Paul Stillwell: Were there any layers in the chain of command between you and General Crist at that point?

Admiral Bernsen: No, that was a very direct relationship, and, in fact, interestingly enough, there were many Navy people who tended to criticize the chain of command as being cumbersome, when indeed it was extremely simple. I think most of those criticisms really were not directed at the cumbersome aspects, but simply at the fact that there was no Navy four-star who was in charge, as there had been in that area up until 1983 when CentCom was born. The understanding within DoD was that CentCom would be commanded either by an Army or Marine general. Interestingly enough, of course, Crist being a Marine officer, was part of the naval establishment. Nevertheless, his position was not something that was considered to be in the Navy chain of command, and that disturbed some of those Navy folks.

Paul Stillwell: Had that area belonged to CinCUSNavEur before CentCom came along?

Admiral Bernsen: Well, in 1979 it actually moved from CinCUSNavEur's area of security and responsibility to CinCPac's.* CinCPac and PacFlt were directly involved as commanders in the area for probably two or three years.† The predecessor of CentCom was the RDJTF, which was formed in 1980 when Lieutenant General P. X. Kelley, a Marine, was in charge.‡ Interestingly enough, in 1980 we ended up with a liaison officer on the staff on the flagship from the RDJTF, but there was no direct opcon relationship between the RDJTF and ComMidEastFor. ComMidEastFor still worked for Pac. That changed in 1983 with the creation of CentCom and has remained the same since.

Paul Stillwell: How much contact did you have with General Crist when you were in that position?

Admiral Bernsen: A great deal of contact with him. Not only did he come and visit on a frequent basis—by that I mean probably once every two to three months at least. But once the tanker war intensified—and I would say that would be the spring of '87—I had a conversation with General Crist on the telephone almost every day. He was very interested in what was going on, and invariably would call in the early evening hours—6:00-7:00 o'clock—and we would chat at length about what was going on and various and sundry actions that we were taking to assert our presence.

Paul Stillwell: Would you characterize that as a harmonious relationship?

Admiral Bernsen: Oh, yes, I think so. Having been his J-5, it was primarily in response to his request that the CNO assigned me as ComMidEastFor. I am absolutely sure had I not been to his liking that that wouldn't have happened. So the relationship was a harmonious one. I always had the impression that, while George Crist certainly had a mind of his own and had some very specific ideas on how CentCom ought to be run, I

---

* CinCUSNavEur – Commander in Chief U.S. Naval Forces Europe; CinCPac – Commander in Chief Pacific, a joint-service command.
† PacFlt – Pacific Fleet.
‡ On 1 March 1980 the United States officially established the Rapid Deployment Joint Task Force, based in Tampa, Florida. On 1 January 1983 it became the U.S. Central Command. Lieutenant General Paul X. Kelley, USMC, later Commandant of the Marine Corps.

think he valued my opinion when it came to naval matters. I think he certainly felt comfortable in the relationship in that in his view, at least, things seemed to be going well in the Gulf and that ships were being deployed properly during the war, etc., etc.

Paul Stillwell: At what point did the staff start building up in response to this series of events?

Admiral Bernsen: Well, I think the thing that changed the whole flavor of the Gulf was the decision to re-flag the tankers.* That isn't to say that things hadn't changed somewhat prior to that, in that both the Iraqis, as well as the Iranians, had increased the number of attacks on shipping and were both more active at sea than they had been before in many different ways. So things had already begun to escalate. And, in fact, the re-flagging of the tankers was in response to that escalation, really, because what had happened was that the Iranians had increased the number and level of attacks against third-country, ostensibly neutral ships.

It was during the latter part of 1986, in the spring of 1987, that it seemed that ships that were bound for Kuwait—regardless of what kind of cargo they carried—seemed to be getting hit by the Iranians more than anybody else's ships, or more than before. Whether it was actually true or not was a little hard to prove, but it seemed so, at least to the Kuwaitis. I think there was probably a pretty good case that could be made that that was true, and I think it made some sense. A great deal of the Iraqi war material was coming in through Kuwaiti ports. A lot of it was coming in through Saudi Arabia overland, and through Aqaba and Jordan overland on the long highway to Baghdad. But a great deal of material—particularly from the Soviet Union and the East Bloc—was coming in on Soviet and East Bloc ships being off-loaded at the terminals in Kuwait and then simply driven overland up to Iraq, which was obviously just a very short distance away.

---

* In the early months of 1987, during a war between Iran and Iraq, each side was attacking tankers in the Persian Gulf. In order to protect the flow of oil in the gulf, the United States re-flagged a number of Kuwaiti commercial tankers to provide them U.S. registry. That enabled the U.S. Navy to escort the tankers in an operation labeled Earnest Will.

So I think the Iranian attacks, on either Kuwaiti-registered ships or ships in trade in Kuwaiti, were a response to that. I think they were attempting in their own way to intimidate the Kuwaitis. The Kuwaitis recognized this and became deeply upset, and felt that if allowed to continue that they would become relatively isolated, particularly in their geographic position up in the northern Gulf. So, as a small nation, particularly a nation with some very cunning leadership, they decided to go and get some help. And instead of just asking one particular country to help them, they asked a bunch of them to help: the Soviets, the United States, as well as the British. The British really didn't want to get involved. I'm not even sure how high level those contacts were, but I do recall the Brits essentially never let it get beyond the request stage, just bolted. We first received a written communication from the Kuwaitis as far back as December 1986.

Paul Stillwell: Now, by we, do you mean Middle East Force?

Admiral Bernsen: No, we being the United States, our government.

Paul Stillwell: Through diplomatic channels.

Admiral Bernsen: That's right. All of this was done through diplomatic channels; I should have been clear on that. There were no proposals made directly to me or anyone else in the Middle East Force. Our government's position, quite frankly, I think, was that we didn't really want to get involved. My read on that came from speaking to a lot of diplomats during that period of time, including Assistant Secretary of State Dick Murphy; Tony Quainton, our ambassador in Kuwait; and our ambassador in Bahrain.[*] And that's a fairly distinct historical position too. The Kuwaitis—although they did buy some airplanes from us a few years ago—really, really have never been very close to us. There have been political and diplomatic differences over the years. I don't think that the United States was particularly interested in getting involved in the tanker war in the Persian Gulf.

---

[*] Richard W. Murphy, a Foreign Service Officer, served as Assistant Secretary of State for Near Eastern and South Asian Affairs from 1983 to 1989. Anthony C. E. Quainton was U.S. Ambassador to Kuwait from September 1984 to August 1987.

Paul Stillwell: Well, we had been an interested bystander for several years already.

Admiral Bernsen: That's right. And now, here were the Kuwaitis asking us to help them. Obviously there were differences of opinion in Washington, but I think the consensus, particularly at the State Department, was that it wasn't a productive exercise to get too involved.

The interesting thing, however, was that the Kuwaitis also approached the Soviet Union. The Soviets were not quite as reluctant, and they began to negotiate almost immediately on what form their assistance would take. This was the backdrop, then, to our own diplomatic position relative to the Kuwaiti.

Paul Stillwell: How was the United States aware of these contacts between the Kuwaitis and the Soviets?

Admiral Bernsen: I'm not really sure, other than I don't think that either side was all that reticent. As I recall, it appeared in the open press, not in detail, but the fact that something was going on. And we began to see more Soviet ships in the Gulf. I don't remember the exact dates, but we began to see Soviet ships, specifically large oceangoing minesweepers, being used as escorts in the Gulf for Kuwaiti-flag ships. They would go up the Gulf to a particular area, and, then they would turn around and go back. But they would, in fact, escort these Kuwaiti ships. I don't remember all the detail on that; I'm not sure how significant it is either. At any rate, spurred on by the fact that there was some competition, we were seeing more and more Soviet ships in the Gulf, where we had never seen them before. They had always been very careful to stay out, because I'm sure they didn't want to antagonize us.

By doing this, the Soviets would certainly increase their standing influence with the Arabs, since Oman had just declared that it was going to establish diplomatic relations with the Soviet Union. The Soviets already had some relations, formal relations, with the UAE, and that there even had been some discussion—I'm not sure how serious—in Saudi Arabia about establishing a relationship with the Soviets. You put all that together, it became particularly clear, I think, to the conservatives in the Reagan administration that we couldn't let the Soviets outmaneuver us, if you will.*

Now, did the Soviets really have a fine-tuned plan? I don't know. But it would be an interesting topic for somebody to look into sometime. I think, perhaps, they sort of felt much like we did.

Paul Stillwell: Did the Soviet naval forces going into the Gulf establish any kind of contact, formal or informal, with you?

Admiral Bernsen: Yes, there was some kind of contact, bridge to bridge, just the normal kind of passing instructions and that sort of thing. But we certainly had no formal contact with them. I did get some guidance from Washington, as I recall, that said, in essence, "Business as usual; we don't encourage you to make a big issue out of this." So we didn't.

Paul Stillwell: Were you asked for any suggestions on how to reply to the Kuwaiti initiatives?

Admiral Bernsen: Yes, General Crist and I discussed the issue at great length on the phone. He wasn't over there at the time, as I recall. Most of it boiled down to not so much whether or not I thought it was diplomatically a good idea. That really wasn't asked of me, but I was asked: Could I do it? How would I do it? How many ships did we need? Was it feasible? Did it make sense from that standpoint? We put the staff to work on that almost immediately.

During those initial planning stages—and now we're talking about probably April of 1987—it became reasonably clear in my mind, certainly clear in others' minds—that getting involved we did run a risk. There was no question about it. The Iranians and Iraqis were shooting each other; if we headed right in the middle of it, it could be very risky. Under those circumstances, one of the things that we really would have liked to have had was access to air power. Then we began to figure out how we were going to do that. It became quickly very clear that that was going to be tough, unless you wanted to

---

* Ronald W. Reagan served as President of the United States from 20 January 1981 to 20 January 1989.

bring an aircraft carrier into the Gulf, and that was something that we did not want to do for a whole host of reasons.

Paul Stillwell: Were the Saudis approached as they were several years later for Desert Shield?*

Admiral Bernsen: You mean as far as basing U.S. aircraft in Saudi?

Paul Stillwell: Yes.

Admiral Bernsen: There was discussion with them, I'm sure. But in those days the Saudis simply didn't feel threatened enough to be prompted to give us air rights. If you threatened the Saudis, then they would jump into your lap, but if things appeared to them to be going relatively normally, then we didn't see that kind of offer.

Paul Stillwell: Do you know where the specific tactic of re-flagging Kuwaiti tankers came from?

Admiral Bernsen: Well, I think that was really decided in Washington. A couple of delegations went to see officials in Kuwaiti. The delegations had among the membership people from the State Department and the Coast Guard. The Coast Guard was very involved. There were a couple of relatively junior officers up in Kuwait that I ran into a couple of times who were involved in the actual mechanics of re-flagging and re-reregistering the Kuwaiti ships.

Paul Stillwell: That's the Coast Guard's business.

---

* In January 1991 U.S. and Allied Coalition forces attacked Iraq to get it to retreat following its August 1990 invasion of neighboring Kuwait. The holding action in the meantime was Operation Desert Shield. The conflict itself became known variously as Operation Desert Storm and the Gulf War. Coalition forces won the war in February 1991.

Admiral Bernsen: The real impetus for the re-flagging was the fact that if we sailed as an escort of a ship carrying a Kuwaiti flag, or some other country, there were some very distinct international rules, implications, that complicated the issue: the protection of third-country nationals, particularly putting our sailors' lives on the line to protect non-U.S. individuals.

Paul Stillwell: Did you have an international law specialist on your staff?

Admiral Bernsen: We did indeed, did indeed, and a very good one, helped me a great deal.

So by actually putting an American flag on the stern, legitimately registering the ship in the United States, we would be protecting an American vessel. Then those international rules, and our own internal rules within our own body of law, became much simpler.

Paul Stillwell: And you also had American lives on board those ships as crew members.

Admiral Bernsen: Oh, yes. Interestingly enough, probably among the biggest early sticking points with the Kuwaiti Oil Tanker Company were negotiations concerning how many Americans had to be aboard these ships. They didn't want any Americans on board, because they had to pay them more. That simple. Our unions wanted the ships manned totally by Americans. We came to an agreement that was someplace in between. What I think it all boiled down to was that the master, the radioman, and the mates were all Americans. The rest of the crew were hodgepodge. But, yes, there definitely were some issues there and some problems.

Paul Stillwell: Were you involved in any of those negotiations?

Admiral Bernsen: No, no, none of those negotiations.

Now, I was very directly involved with the Kuwaiti Emir, Prime Minister, Defense Minister, and our ambassador to Kuwait on the details of how the escort operation would run, where we would go, how many ships we would escort, what routes they would take, where we would pick them up, drop them off—the detail arrangements that were all part of that game. One issue was compensatory fuel. The Kuwaitis agreed to provide fuel to our escort vessels, but how it was to be done took time to sort out. Interesting sidelight here was the fact that the Kuwaitis were not particularly anxious for our escort ships to come into port. That got out in the news and became quite a bone of contention in the U.S. papers. Here we were protecting their ships, but they didn't want us to come into port.

Well, I think it got a little bit out of proportion. It came up again later on when we were dickering for helicopter platforms and such. The Kuwaitis were accused of being ingrates, because we couldn't base helicopters in Kuwait. The fact of the matter is, although they were ingrates to some extent, the helicopter thing wasn't very bothersome, because had the helicopters been based ashore, they wouldn't have really been able to cover the area that we wanted to cover. It was too great a distance for them to fly to the area at sea that needed coverage. So that was never really a concern. We, in fact, never asked the Kuwaitis to base Navy helicopters ashore.

Paul Stillwell: Did you ask them to let you bring ships into their ports?

Admiral Bernsen: The question only came up relative to where we would fuel them. They wanted to do it by barge, and I wasn't really averse to that. It really was a bit of a tempest in a teapot; it wasn't really one of those big issues. From the point of saving face or diplomatically, certainly it had some ramifications. But relative to the operation itself, it really didn't make a hill of beans one way or the other.

But what did happen was that I made two or three visits to Kuwait. One was with Admiral Crowe.* In fact, that was the first direct visit where Admiral Crowe was the United States Government's Defense Department's direct emissary to the Emir and the members of the government, where he actually told them that we would, in fact, escort their ships, and basically how we were going to do it. It was, I must admit, a fairly

---

* Admiral William J. Crowe, Jr., USN, served as Chairman of the Joint Chiefs of Staff from 1 October 1985 to 30 September 1989.

general discussion, because at that point in time—I think that was April of '87—we didn't really know exactly what we were going to do. It wasn't until May, the next month, that we had a number of planning meetings in which we really figured out exactly how we were going to do it. So when he gave his assurances to the Kuwaitis, there was still some fumbling around. In fact, a short time previously Crowe had come to Bahrain, had been on the flagship, where we sat down and worked out a plan that then became acceptable to CentCom and to Washington.

That plan was then elaborated on and modified, and the next major planning session was between me and the carrier group commander who was sitting in the North Arabian Sea in the late spring of '87. That was Admiral Lyle Bull, who came to Bahrain, actually.* We sat with members of his staff, members of my staff, and a couple of officers, as I recall, from CentCom. We sat down and basically did it. There was a straw man that had been brought over from CentCom, which was essentially the same plan that we had sent them. So it all sort of came together, and I'm not too sure that if you asked anybody today who was it that authored the plan, that anybody could really tell you with any degree of certainty.

Paul Stillwell: So a fair amount of brainstorming at various levels.

Admiral Bernsen: Oh, yes, a lot of brainstorming at various levels, and, of course, the reason Bull was there was to make sure we had air cover. The air cover would extend up into the Strait of Hormuz, and under extraordinary circumstances the plan stipulated that aircraft could be flown deeply into the Gulf. So if one of our ships came under attack, we could call for air power. Now, it was going to be tough to get them there; we were going to have to tank some airplanes. But, at least in theory, we could get fighter-attack airplanes two-thirds of the way up the Gulf in about 30 minutes. Now, if you're out there getting shot at, 30 minutes is a long time. You're probably going to get shot pretty bad, but maybe the guy that shot you is not going to get away—particularly if it's a surface ship. Now if it's another airplane, that might be something else again.

---

* Rear Admiral Lyle F. Bull, USN, Commander Carrier Group Seven.

So it wasn't a perfect arrangement. I mean, from my point of view, it would have been a hell of a lot better if the carrier could have moved up into the Gulf of Oman a bit more closely, and if we had had authorization to fly directly across the Musandam Peninsula, which came later, by the way; but initially it was all pretty dicey stuff.* Lyle was going to do the best he could, but he couldn't promise a hell of a lot. And we didn't have any Air Force tanking assets in Saudi Arabia. Again, that came later too.

Paul Stillwell: Was it pretty mechanical as far as the surface ship escorts?

Admiral Bernsen: Well, on paper it looked mechanical. I'm not too sure that it was very mechanical for the guys who were doing it. In fact, initially, it wasn't mechanical at all, because one of the things that we found right off the bat was that 100,000-200,000-ton tankers don't maneuver like warships. The way we set up the escort format, we had a warship in the lead, and he might maneuver violently, let's say, including coming to all-stop. In that case, the 100,000-200,000-ton tankers would run right up the escort's butt, because the tanker couldn't stop that quickly, and he couldn't maneuver to get out of the way.

That difficulty was really compounded because we had more than one tanker in a row. The guy who was number two or number three had a real problem with all this. In fact, we almost had a couple of collisions. So the problem initially was not Iranians or anyone else; it was how to get this whole thing orchestrated in such a way that we weren't going to kill each other. This whole business started in July of 1987. Right from the beginning, after the first incident or two where we were almost hitting our own people, that was when the decision was made to put a U.S. Naval Reserve officer on board each of the tankers to act as sort of a liaison and a pilot.

Paul Stillwell: They were from the naval control of shipping organization.

Admiral Bernsen: Yes. In fact, they did a super job throughout the war under some very difficult circumstances. But they were there so that we didn't collide. They didn't take

---

* The Musandam Peninsula juts into the Strait of Hormuz from the Arabian Peninsula.

control of the ships specifically, but they briefed the masters on characteristics of warships, and they became the operation's continuity. They transferred from ship to ship to ship, and made multiple trips.

Paul Stillwell: Going back to Admiral Crowe, was he personally involved just because of his stature as Chairman and his previous experience as your predecessor?[*]

Admiral Bernsen: Well, I think that was certainly part of it. I think he would have been involved had he never been Middle East Force, simply because from a military standpoint it was the crisis of the time. And it was a crisis that in Admiral Crowe's point of view needed to be handled very carefully so that we weren't going to get into something we didn't want to get into. While I don't want to editorialize on the political reasons for the war, certainly one of the reasons we were not there was to go to war with Iran—or Iraq, for that matter—but certainly not with Iran. So we wanted to walk a rather thin line here.

We were trying to form a buffer, a deterrent so that the war wouldn't widen, so that our oil-producing friends in the Gulf wouldn't be unduly pressured, so that the oil would continue to flow. We weren't doing a very good job at that, because obviously lots of ships were getting hit. But it was that fine line. How far were we going to go to put pressure on Iran, short of going to war with Iran? And it wasn't just the oil business. Iran did form a buffer with the Soviet Union in 1986-87. Certainly the Soviet Union was still in our view a great threat. We didn't want to cause so much instability in Iran that the government folded up, and as a result we ended up with chaos in Iran, which would offer the Soviets even more opportunities for mischief-making than they had perhaps back during the Mosaddeq era.[†]

So there was a whole block of underlying difficulties here—rocks and shoals that had to be navigated. Crowe had been out there before and had also, I think, become one of the recognized political-military experts in our government.

---

[*] As a rear admiral Crowe served as Commander Middle East Force from 30 June 1976 to 4 July 1977.
[†] Mohammed Mosaddeq was the elected Prime Minister of Iran from 1951 to 1953. The U.S. Central Intelligence Agency was involved in a coup that overthrew his government. At that time the Shah became the head of the Iranian Government.

Paul Stillwell: And in OP-06.*

Admiral Bernsen: But more than just the Chairman of the Joint Chiefs, he was a real politician sailor, if you will; he was the ideal guy. He did understand the people as best you can do that, although his information was outdated, and, in fact, quite outdated in some respects.

Paul Stillwell: Do you have any examples of that?

Admiral Bernsen: Well, I don't want to make a big issue out of that. It was simply that the relationship had changed. When he commanded the Middle East Force, the Shah was in power, and Iran was a great friend.† That's what I mean. So he had to get acclimatized to the new political reality, because what was going on in the Gulf was totally at variance from his experience. During his tour there wasn't anybody shooting, and there weren't any tankers blowing up and all that sort of thing. The Iraqis weren't flying airplanes around. In fact, in the mid-'70s, they probably didn't have any airplanes to fly. So it was very different. But he did have a basic and innate feel for Arabs, negotiating with Arabs, and what they were all about. I think that's important.

Paul Stillwell: Did he have some residual personal relationships that helped?

Admiral Bernsen: Yes, he did in Bahrain. I don't think he had in any of the other countries. But he certainly did in Bahrain. I think it was late '86, when he came back to Bahrain on his tenth anniversary as Middle East Force and was presented with a medal by the Emir. He hadn't been there in ten years, so that was his first trip back. I happened to be there at the time, and I spent a day or two with him, went around on a number of his calls, in fact spent a lot of time talking about Bahrain and the Gulf.

---

* Vice Admiral Crowe served as Deputy Chief of Naval Operations (Plans, Policy and Operations) from August 1977 to March 1980.
† Mohammad Reza Pahlavi (1919-1980) became Shah of Iran (or Persia, as it was then known) in 1941 and held office until his regime was ousted in 1979 by the Ayatollah Khomeini.

He came back again just a few months later when we began to develop this tanker-escort business. Then the two of us ended up going to Kuwait together. There were three instances within a period of six months, so we spent some time together talking about this. And then in June of 1987, perhaps one of the most interesting aspects of all of this, we were just about to put the plan into effect. Everybody was on board, we had selected the ships that were going to be escorted, we had the escorts in place, the number of ships in the force that had been augmented; we then had eight. And we obviously were getting prepared in many other ways as well, not knowing what the reaction of the Iranians would be.

Then I got a message from Admiral Crowe that said basically, "I'd like you to come up to Germany." I think the occasion was CinCEur's change of command, and Crowe was coming over from Washington.* He said, "I'm going to be in Germany; I'm going to send an airplane down there for you, and you come up to Stuttgart," as I recall, "and we'll chat about what's going to happen."

I went up there. I don't remember the exact day in June, not that it makes too much difference. I would say we were about ten days or two weeks away from actually going into the escort business. I flew up there and met with him in—I think it was in Deputy CinCEur's house, a house I had been in before, interestingly enough, some years before. But it was in the study, and it started off just him and me and a colonel who was his EA, who was taking lots of notes.† We began by simply going over the operation as it was planned, the forces that I had available, communications links, intelligence, whatever else, and then he began to ask me, "What if? Okay, you know, what if this happens, what do you do? What if this happens, what are you going to do?" I would answer the best I could. But I'll be quite honest, I had prepared for that, so I had some answers. They may not have been good answers, but I had answers.

Paul Stillwell: Do you remember any of the what ifs?

---

* CinCEur – Commander in Chief U.S. Forces Europe.
† EA – executive assistant.

Admiral Bernsen: Oh, yes, I remember a number of the what ifs. One in particular became indeed prophetic. It was, "What if you catch an Iranian laying mines?"

I remember my answer, which was, "That violates international law, and if he doesn't stop on command, we will stop him by using force, and I'm authorized to do that. Agreed?" Admiral Crowe's position was that that was quite correct. If you go and look at accepted International Law—in the ROE at that time that we were operating under, there were certain provisions that allowed you to drop mines in your own territorial waters for defensive purposes.[*] But if someone is dropping mines in international waters, under our interpretation of the Law, they are performing an illegal act, an aggressive act, an act of war in essence, and you have the obligation and the right to stop such activity. So we were very clear on that point. He agreed that if I encountered an Iranian laying mines in international waters, I wasn't going to have to get any permission from higher authority to stop him. If in fact we came upon an Iranian laying mines and he did not stop upon command or in fact, we didn't even command him, we just stopped him. As far as Admiral Crowe was concerned, that was the right course of action.

It was a very significant point, because of course we in fact came upon just such an occasion later in the summer when the *Iran Ajr* was caught in the middle of the night.[†] We took the *Iran Ajr* under fire, which turned out to be a very simple operation from a command-and-control point of view, because the attacking helicopters were under direct control of the frigate.[‡] The frigate was in direct radio contact with the flagship, and in fact my operations officer was on the other end of the radio circuit, and I was standing next to him.

Paul Stillwell: This was Captain Grieve?[§]

---

[*] ROE – rules of engagement.
[†] *Iran Ajr* was a 614-ton, 177-foot-long steel-hulled landing craft/minelayer used by Iran during the Iran-Iraq War. On the night of 21 September 1987, while the ship was in the process of laying mines in shipping lanes in the central Persian Gulf, she was attacked by AH-6 Army helicopters after surveillance by an MH-6 Army helicopter. The mining operation ceased, and the next morning U.S. Navy and Marine teams boarded and captured the disabled ship, which was later sunk by explosive charges in a deep-water location of the Gulf.
[‡] The frigate, on which the Army helicopters were based, was the USS *Jarrett* (FFG-33).
[§] Captain David J. Grieve, USN, a surface warfare officer.

Admiral Bernsen: That's right. We had been tracking the *Iran Ajr* for two or three days. When the Army helicopter pilots reported that the Iranians were dropping "mine-like objects," we had enough intelligence to recognize that the mine-like objects were really mines. The pilots wanted to know what to do, and that request was immediately relayed to Captain Grieve. I was able to very quickly give the order to take the Iranians under fire. That whole sequence back and forth took something like 60 to 90 seconds; it was very quick.

So we didn't have to stop and try and get CentCom or Washington or somebody on a super high frequency and go through all that garbled nonsense and all the rest of it. It had already been discussed, and I felt very comfortable with that decision, because not two weeks before Admiral Crowe had told me specifically, "Yeah, that's exactly what your job is, and if you find a situation, why, that's what you do." I'm not sure that everyone felt as comfortable as I did, but I did, and at the time that was what counted, because I was the officer who was giving the order.

Paul Stillwell: Do you remember any of the other what ifs?

Admiral Bernsen: Yes. What if an Iranian starts shooting at one of the escort vessels? And, of course, that was pretty clear as well, spelled out in the ROE. If somebody starts shooting at you, you can start shooting back. There were a lot of what ifs relative to the definition of an aggressive act, a threatening act. What does an Iranian aircraft have to do in order for him to be considered threatening, things interestingly enough that probably related, to some extent at least, to the shoot-down of the Iranian airliner much later.[*] But I wasn't around for that. Not that it would have made any difference. I'm not suggesting that Admiral Less made a mistake, because he really didn't have an option.[†] That was

---

[*] On 3 July 1988, Iran Air flight 655, an A300 airbus en route from Bandar Abbas Airport to Dubai, United Arab Emirates, was destroyed by two SM-2 Standard missiles launched at a range of nine miles by the Aegis cruiser *Vincennes* (CG-49). All 290 persons on board the civilian airliner died.
[†] Rear Admiral Anthony A. Less, USN, became Commander Middle East Force/Joint Task Force Middle East in a change of command ceremony on 27 February 1988. The event was on board the USS *Coronado* (AGF-11), which then became flagship of the combined force.

something that the ship's skipper had the responsibility for.* I think it was just generally a whole series of what ifs relative to the things that most likely might happen.

The one "what if" I don't remember, and I must admit that this may be because it was not discussed, or because I didn't think it was important enough at the time, was what if you hit a mine? I'm just not sure that that one came up. Yet it probably should have, because in June we had already received good intelligence on the fact that the Iranians—or somebody, my assumption being the Iranians—had laid mines in the Al Ahmadi Channel off Kuwait. Now, that is the channel that goes almost at right angles to the beach, out to sea from the oil refineries in Kuwait. It's not a channel that we were going to go into on the escort mission. We were going to drop off the Kuwaiti ships considerably to the south of that channel. But what didn't occur, to me certainly, was a real connection between that mining and Iranian intentions with regard to us.

My interpretation of those mines off Kuwait in that channel was that they were directed at some other ships but not at U.S. warships, because U.S. warships weren't going up there. That was probably a much too rigid interpretation, as I look back on it, because when you put mines in a channel, you can't predict who's going to be the target. I'm not sure the Iranians knew that we weren't going to go up and down there. We could very well have sent a warship as far as they knew. So, really, when I look back on it, I think I interpreted the mining incident much too restrictively, when in fact by the mere act of laying mines in the Al Ahmadi Channel, the Iranians had already declared that they were willing to use mines against anyone, including the U.S. Navy.

There's another conclusion that I think you could draw from that. Maybe this is too broad a conclusion, I don't know, but I thought about it a great deal. I think it was during this period of time—April, May, June—that the Iranian leadership literally must have sat down around a table, Rafsanjani and the rest of them, and consciously made a decision that they were willing to risk U.S. retaliatory air power.† You know, up until that time, we always thought that the deterrent U.S. military power would prevent the

---

* Captain William C. Rogers III, USN, commanded the Aegis cruiser *Vincennes* (CG-49) from 11 April 1987 to 27 May 1989. He and his wife Sharon wrote a book titled *Storm Center: A Personal Account of Tragedy & Terrorism* (Annapolis: Naval Institute Press, 1992).
† Akbar Hashemi Rafsanjani was chairman of the Iranian Parliament and de facto commander in chief of the armed forces from 1980 to 1989.

Iranians from carrying out a purposeful attack on our forces. In the early '80s, '80-'81, we put the aircraft carrier in the Indian Ocean as a deterrent. The idea was that the Iranians would not attack either us or an ally, because they were so afraid they would be blown away by carrier air. But I think in April and May the situation had gotten so difficult for the Iranians relative to Iraq that they decided—made a conscious decision—to take the risk. "We cannot let this escort operation go on unchallenged," I think was the decision. "We cannot let the Iraqis blow up all of our ships." By that time Iranian exports were down to 500,000 barrels a day from a high of over two million. The Iraqis were flying their French fighter and attack aircraft all the way down the Gulf and dropping bombs right outside Bandar Abbas, the areas where the tankers would get together and consolidate.* It was really vicious.

I think the Iranians at that point had made up their mind and decided, "Okay, we're going to go attack somebody. We're going to sink a ship, and it might very well be an American warship. And if we do, we're probably going to get attacked by carrier air. They're probably going to bomb Bandar Abbas or some other city or important installation, and that's okay. It's not okay, but we'll risk it—we are willing to risk it." That was a sea change in their whole way of thinking, because up until then I don't believe the Iranians wanted to risk that. But I think they had been forced into the corner, were in such desperate straits from their point of view, that they were actually willing to risk being attacked—full-blown attack—by the U.S. Navy's carriers. I'm also not convinced that it was a unanimous decision. And because of events that took place later on, I tend to be convinced that perhaps one of the guys who didn't agree with this was Rafsanjani himself.

Paul Stillwell: Why do you say that?

Admiral Bernsen: Well, in April '88, after I had left the Gulf and turned over to Rear Admiral Less, we ended up with the big Praying Mantis dust-up, where we actually went

---

* Bandar Abbas is an Iranian port city in the southern Persian Gulf.

in with carrier air and blew up a couple of their ships.[*] It was at that time that Rafsanjani took over as essentially the head of the government.[†] I really believe that he was the guy—not a moderating influence, but basically an opportunist who said, "This isn't getting us anywhere. They just blew up what navy we had; this is dumb." And I'm not sure that Rafsanjani was really keen on conducting an obvious and visible attack on a U.S. military asset. Bluff, yes, maybe even mine a ship perhaps, but if it doesn't work, then you better back off.

Paul Stillwell: Well, there must have been a hierarchy of risk, though, because they would try a mine but not shoot a Silkworm at a U.S. combatant ship, for example.[‡]

Admiral Bernsen: Well, that's right in hindsight. And now it all looks relatively logical. I'm not sure it was all that logical; I'm really not. I think sometimes we may draw too many conclusions from that sort of thing. Yes, there were certainly some decisions. And, again, I want to emphasize that I think there were some basic decisions that were made by the head of the government and the very top individuals literally, sitting around a table. In other words, it was not all fragmented. There wasn't one guy doing one thing off in the corner and another guy doing something else. You did have the basic division between the armed forces, the regular armed forces, and the Revolutionary Guard. Although there were times when you weren't too sure who was in the driver's seat.

I think by the time Rafsanjani took over as boss it was clear that the Revolutionary Guards had lost influence, and a more normal approach to the world was in the ascendancy. That isn't to say that Rafsanjani is a good guy. Absolutely not. He is an opportunist of the first order, cunning, ruthless as hell, but I think he is at least a relatively practical guy, and he was not interested in getting into a war with us either.

---

[*] Operation Praying Mantis took place in the Persian Gulf on 18 April 1988 as retaliation for the Iranian mining that led to damage of the frigate *Samuel B. Roberts* (FFG-58) on 14 April. The U.S. attack was mounted by surface combatants inside the Gulf and planes from the aircraft carrier *Enterprise* (CVN-65), which was in the North Arabian Sea. Irani losses from Praying Mantis included one frigate sunk, one gunboat sunk, three speedboats sunk, one frigate damaged, and two oil platforms damaged. For details, see Michael A. Palmer, "Operation Praying Mantis," in Jack Sweetman, editor, *Great American Naval Battles* (Annapolis: Naval Institute Press, 1998), pages 381-399.
[†] Rafsanjani served as President of Iran from 3 August 1989 to 2 August 1997.
[‡] Silkworm is a Chinese-made antiship missile.

Whereas I think some of the revolutionaries and the clerics, for whatever reason, likely religious fanaticism, weren't adverse to saying, "That's okay. And if we go to war with them, fine. We'll kill them too." You know, that sort of thing.

Paul Stillwell: Did you have any internal intelligence on what was going on in Iran?

Admiral Bernsen: Damn little. Oh, sure, there was some reporting, but it was very difficult to ferret out specific details concerning leadership decision-making. And I'm not sure that anybody had that kind of detail, quite frankly. I never saw any report, and certainly no report to be authoritative anyway. So what you really did was you sort of made your assumptions based on what you knew about them, their track record, which was very important.

You went all the way back to '80 and looked at how these guys functioned, how they related to the Iraqis and how they had related to the allies, the Brits, and the other Gulf countries, and you formed certain opinions. Quite frankly, it was one of the most irritating parts of the exercise, to welcome the itinerant news writer, journalist, who might be a very smart, very astute guy and a hell of a good writer with absolutely no background on the Gulf, who simply didn't have that understanding of how things had progressed. And without that context, they were just throwing darts at the walls as to what the hell was going on. But those of us who had some knowledge of how the Iranians operated and their track record in the Gulf, I think were a lot better position to figure out what they were going to do and what was really important and what wasn't.

At any rate, to complete the thought. They had made a conscious decision to risk the wrath of the United States when they laid those mines in Al Ahmadi, and then, of course—no question about it—to get the first convoy.*

Bridgeton, the biggest ship of all, which was also somewhat ironic, came steaming up the Gulf. As you will recall, there was a tremendous amount of media interest, and we had reporters on the escort ships. I mean, it was a circus, and there were

---

* The merchant ships in the convoy were the 401,000-ton tanker *Bridgeton* and the 48,233-ton *Gas Prince*. Escorts were the cruiser *Fox* (CG-33), destroyer *Kidd* (DDG-993), and frigate *Crommelin* (FFG-37). The convoy began its northward journey from the anchorage at Khor Fakkan in the Gulf of Oman on the morning of 22 July 1987. It then proceeded through the Strait of Hormuz into the Persian Gulf.

a lot of people who were very concerned about the fact that it was a circus. Crowe, I know, was just very ticked. I don't know that I was totally calm. We all had mixed emotions. Should we have the reporters on board? Should this be a media event? Shouldn't it be? But you remember that up until that very moment when the *Bridgeton* hit a mine near Farsi Island, we had approached the Iranians in a very interesting way.* We were not at war with them.† They had not shot at us. The principal thing that we were interested in was deconfliction of the Iranians.‡ So we not only didn't shoot at them, and they didn't shoot at us, but we told them where we were all the time. It was a very open relationship.

We had our little ROE where if you saw an Iranian airplane, or you saw them on radar or visually, you called them on the radio and said, "This is an American ship. Stay away. And if you come any closer I'll shoot you." That sort of thing. And when you do that, obviously, you give yourself away, because that's what we wanted to do. We put this little glass cocoon around ourselves; we did that by communicating. And it was so funny, because when new ships would come into the Gulf in those days, part of the mindset that we had to change was the way we normally practice in a blue-water environment, where everybody's in emcon.§ Nobody says anything, and you don't have your radar turned on, and I would get those guys on the flagship and say, "Now look, you've got to get your mind right here. You've got to have your radars on, you've got to tell the Iranians where you are, blah-blah-blah-blah. It's a totally different world."

Well, here we were, steaming up the Gulf; everybody was telling everybody where they were. My God, they had a little line on television back home, tracing the route of the convoy.

Paul Stillwell: So you believed that the very presence of the escorts would serve as a

---

* The re-flagged super tanker *Bridgeton* was damaged by an Iranian mine on the morning of 24 July 1987. The ship's master was Captain Frank C. Seitz Jr., U.S. Merchant Marine. For an interview with Seitz about the incident, see, "SS *Bridgeton*: The First Convoy, *U.S. Naval Institute Proceedings*, May 1988, page 52.
† Farsi Island, in the northern part of the Persian Gulf, is the site of an Iranian naval base.
‡ Deconfliction involved setting up procedures whereby ships and aircraft could communicate with each other and thus, presumably, avoid hostilities based on mistaken identification.
§ Emcon – emission control, that is, limiting or eliminating electronic emissions by ships or aircraft.

deterrent?

Admiral Bernsen: Presence of the escorts, the fact that we had the carrier battle group off the coast—all those things taken together were going to deter the Iranians from attacking that convoy. Did I believe in that? Yes, I believed in it; I really did, and I'll admit that. I really did not think that the Iranians were going to lay mines on me.

Was I totally confident about it? No. But in the final analysis I really didn't think they would mine the area through which our ships would pass. Because I still thought that the carrier was an ultimate deterrent when it came to the Iranians. I thought we had made it very clear to them that, by God, if they did something like that, if they hit an American ship—I'm not sure we made it clear to them if they hit a tanker—but I think we made it pretty clear to them in many different ways that if they blew up an American ship that caused loss of life to American sailors, that they were in deep trouble. That meant very simply we were going to take some retaliatory actions—serious. So I thought that was still the operative thing.

Now, what really happened that morning is perhaps the most fascinating part of this whole thing. We had planned the route very carefully so that the majority of it was in daylight. And when it was nighttime, we would either stop the convoy, or we would be in water that was relatively benign, over which we had good control. We wouldn't be in shallow water; we wouldn't be in small restricted areas; we wouldn't be next to an Iranian landmass. As a result, when the ships arrived just northeast of Bahrain in the middle of the night, we stopped them there. We did not get them under way again until almost light the next morning. About 2:00 or 3:00 o'clock in the morning—I take it back. That was a tactic that came a little later in the year. We were continuing to steam them, but I think slowly. But about 2:00 or 3:00 o'clock in the morning, as they were passing northeast of Bahrain, we got some intelligence that indicated that there was some Iranian activity on Farsi Island.

The consensus of the staff—and I agreed—was that what we most likely were looking at was some small-boat activity. There had been a lot of small boats operating in that area, attacking merchant ships, for a long time. The small boats were no match for our escorts, really under any circumstance, but there was always a chance in the middle of the night that they might conceivably sneak up on you and maybe get off a shot or a missile or whatever and kill a couple of guys. That's about all they were going to be able to do, but, of course, we were in a mode that said if one U.S. sailor gets killed, public opinion is going to go crazy.

So I made a decision to slow the whole bunch down so that we would pass Farsi Island in daylight. Well, they did, about 7:30 in the morning, and that's when *Bridgeton* hit the mine, a reckless thing obviously, what all that activity was about. Because that's when the Iranians literally put the mines in their little shallow landing craft and went out and laid the mines. It was that same night, about four hours before *Bridgeton* hit the mine, that the Iranians put the mines in the water. And we didn't recognize it. We just made the wrong choice, absolutely made the wrong choice.

The other aspect of this is—the aspect that is so important—is that the Iranians had absolutely no idea what ship they were going to get with a mine. It could just as well have been the *Kidd* as it was the *Bridgeton*. And, in fact, more likely, because the escort was ahead. It was absolutely only by the grace of God that they didn't hit a U.S. warship. *Bridgeton* was just luck of the draw.

Paul Stillwell: The timing is the basis for your statement; it had to be a conscious decision on their part.

Admiral Bernsen: Oh, yes. That's the point. Absolutely. I mean, they just didn't lay mines out there to harass third-country shipping. Those mines were laid to get one of the ships in that escort—in that convoy. And my bet is that they really put the mines in there to get a U.S. warship and that really they were disappointed when they hit the *Bridgeton*, because, of course, the *Bridgeton*, being almost the biggest tanker in the world, 450,000 tons or whatever it was, could withstand that mine. Whereas, they were large mines, and as witness *Samuel B. Roberts* the next spring, we damn near lost that ship, and we certainly could have lost the *Kidd*.*

Paul Stillwell: One thing I remember asking you when we met on board the *La Salle* was, "What do you think would have happened if the *Kidd* had hit a mine?"

Your very dramatic answer was, "I would have been fired."

Admiral Bernsen: Oh, yes, yes. I don't think there would have been any way in the world that the Navy or the Chairman could have possibly kept me out there if they wanted to. I think the hue and cry would have become just incredible. It was pretty bad as it was.

Paul Stillwell: Did you feel that pressure?

Admiral Bernsen: Not directly. I only felt it because I personally was disappointed. I personally sat down for some hours after the incident and concluded, based on what we had and the facts, that the Al Ahmadi Channel mining should have been a wakeup call, holy smoke; we should have known that. Now, that isn't to say that we just never thought about mines at all; we did. Of course, we did. We had been thinking about mines for sometime. We knew the Iranians had the capability to lay mines. They had laid other mines in the Gulf. The Al Ahmadi Channel wasn't the only place they laid mines. They had floating mines all over the place. So mines were something that we had certainly thought about, and we had taken steps to put into motion the minesweepers coming into the Gulf and all the rest of it.

The escort mission—symbolically, if nothing else—was so important from a political standpoint that we weren't going to wait to have all that equipment in place, minesweepers and all that. That decision was not my decision. That was a decision

---

* On 14 April 1988, the frigate *Samuel B. Roberts* (FFG-58) incurred extensive damage when she ran into and set off an Iranian naval mine in the central Persian Gulf. It took hours of effort on the part of the crew to save the ship from sinking. She received temporary repairs in Dubai and was later returned to the United States for rebuilding. For details see Bradley Peniston, *No Higher Honor: Saving the USS Samuel B. Roberts in the Persian Gulf* (Annapolis: Naval Institute Press, 2006).

made in Washington. Yes, I was asked by General Crist, "What do you think? Are they going to lay mines?"

"I'd like to have some minesweepers here; that'd be real neat. Then we could go sweep the channel, and we'd *know* we weren't going to get hit by mines. But I don't think we're going to get hit by mines."

Paul Stillwell: My memory, possibly shaky, is that the minesweepers didn't start getting in there until after the *Bridgeton* incident.

Admiral Bernsen: Well, I think you're right. However, there had been some talk and discussion and planning and what have you. It was one of those things that should have been included in the initial list of pre-escort "to-do" item. I think the feeling was if we could get away with this thing, just do this escort without having to deploy all these guys, that would be fine. But there had been discussion about it: "What should we do in the event there's mining?" In retrospect we obviously should have had them on the way long before. They still wouldn't have gotten there if we had adhered to our schedule the way it went down in early July. They wouldn't have been there no matter how early we had started them, literally. But we would have been a little bit ahead of the game. As it was, then we had to do some pretty wild improvising, and, of course, the way we did that is we flew some mechanical minesweeping gear in on a C-5.[*] I got together with my Kuwaiti friends at the Kuwaiti Oil Tanker Company. They gave me a couple of offshore servicing boats. We put the mechanical minesweep gear on them. And, of course, the rest is history.

We swept the channel and had these guys do their job. Now, were they really effective? I mean, did they really sweep the channel? I think they did the mechanical mines, although I'm not sure if they ever actually swept them out. But they gave everyone a lot of good feelings, and I think had there been a mechanical mine literally where they were going, I think they probably would have had a good chance to sweep.

---

[*] The C-5 Galaxy is a jet-powered Air Force cargo plane, among the world's largest aircraft.

Paul Stillwell: How soon did the H-53s get into the picture, the helicopter minesweepers?

Admiral Bernsen: That's where I'm a little bit hazy on dates. But I believe they arrived on August 14 on board the *Guadalcanal*. I remember the whole sequence of events very well. They were in Diego Garcia. They off-loaded the Marines, put the MH-53s on board, rolled off from Diego Garcia, literally under cover of darkness, and through the Strait of Hormuz and arrived off Bahrain with nobody knowing about it.[*]

Paul Stillwell: This was in an LPH.

Admiral Bernsen: *Guadalcanal*, with nobody knowing about it, least of all the Iranians.[†] They went through the Strait of Hormuz, darkened ship and the whole business, and there they were. So we had the helicopters. That was quite an operation. I think the guys who were involved did a masterful job; I really do. And there was in fact a lot of conjecture that if the Iranians knew that these things were coming and they could see the *Guadalcanal* coming through the Strait of Hormuz, and they knew what those helicopters were for, that they may well have taken action. So there were all sorts of carrier air in the vicinity, and a darkened ship, as I said, through the strait in the middle of the night. The Iranians never did anything.

I think once the *Bridgeton* hit the mine, and they didn't get the *Kidd*, I think that was certainly a disappointment to the Iranians. Again, I didn't think so at the time. I still hadn't come to grips with the fact that the Iranians weren't really trying to get the tankers. They were trying to get us. It really took a little while for that to totally penetrate, because it was a totally different mindset from six years earlier.

---

[*] The Sikorsky H-53 Sea Stallion is an assault transport helicopter. Deliveries to the fleet began in mid-1966. The helo has a rotor diameter of 72 feet, 3 inches; length, 88 feet, 2 inches; normal takeoff weight, 35,000 pounds; top speed, 196 miles per hour. The CH-53A Sea Stallion was used for minesweeping in the early 1970s, succeeded by the RH-53D Sea Stallion in 1972 and by the MH-53E Sea Dragon since then.

[†] USS *Guadalcanal* (LPH-7), an *Iwo Jima*-class amphibious assault ship, was commissioned 20 July 1963. She was 602 feet long, 84 feet in the beam, extreme width of 105 feet, maximum draft of 29 feet, had a standard displacement of 18,000 tons, and a top speed of 24 knots. She remained in service until decommissioned on 31 August 1994.

Paul Stillwell: What changed your mind on that point?

Admiral Bernsen: I think I just recognized after a few days—or a few hours, for that matter—holy smoke, they didn't know what they were going to hit. And they were really out for anybody, and that meant us too. But then, of course, that incident with the *Bridgeton* was followed not very long after by the incident where they laid the mines outside the Strait of Hormuz and off Fujairah.* And that was a classic, because I think it's one of the few times in any kind of a conflict where you can point to a specific piece of intelligence information and say, "There it is," and then take action on it and be successful. It again illustrated the business of context and continuity and studying and looking at how they operate.

A piece of intelligence information fell into our hands that indicated that the Iranians were going to mine. That particular piece of intel was known in Washington, was known at CentCom, and I knew it as well. It was a piece of national intelligence. In that particular bit of information it stated that the action—mining or whatever—was going to take place in the "anchorage." Well, everybody—certainly everybody at CentCom, General Crist included, was convinced that wherever it was they were going to do, this was in the Gulf. But the only place that we normally referred to as the "anchorage" was off Fujairah. That's where we would actually gather the tankers. They would anchor there for a period of time, and the escorts would pick them up there.

I became convinced very quickly that that was the place that they were going to do it. Nobody believed that, and I mean nobody. Nobody believed that. The reason they didn't was that, again, we had gotten into this mindset that said the Iranians don't want to enlarge this thing; they want to keep it inside the Gulf. Now, we had a whole bunch of reasons why they wouldn't go outside to Fujairah. Oman was their friend. You were talking about putting mines in basically Omani territorial waters. It was outside the Gulf; it was escalation that the Iranians would not do—I mean, the whole list.

Well, I think what I was seeing was that with the *Bridgeton,* all of those kinds of rational things were no longer part of the Iranian mindset. They had already made up

---

* Fujairah is one of the seven members of the United Arab Emirates. It is the only one with a coastline completely on the Gulf of Oman and not in the Persian Gulf. The anchorage is Khor Fakkan, where the *Bridgeton* convoy had formed up prior to its trip into the Gulf.

their mind that they were going to do something to us, and all those niceties had sort of gone out the window. All the conservative thinking didn't make sense anymore. They were going to pick the place that they figured they could get us. Where did those Americans hang out? Well, the place we hung out was that anchorage.

Well, it literally came to me, honest to God, in the middle of the night. I remember getting ahold of the ops boss and saying, "I want a message right now. I want you to get on the radio, and I want every ship out of there." And that's what happened. And I'll be damned if the next day an Iranian ship ran into a mine in that anchorage. Then we later on, of course, pieced it all together, and we knew. We found out when they laid them, the pattern they laid them in, and they literally missed us by 12 hours.

Paul Stillwell: Why would an Iranian ship go in there?

Admiral Bernsen: They didn't talk to those guys; this was their merchant ship.

Paul Stillwell: Oh, a merchant ship.

Admiral Bernsen: A tanker. They weren't talking to the tankers, which, of course, was the ironic part of this whole thing. But Crist had called—or I had called him, I don't remember which—in the middle of the night after I had come to this conclusion and wanted to know what I thought about all this. I said, "I think that's where the Iranians are going to lay their mines."

I got a lot of, "Well, gee, I don't know, you know, why do you think that?" So I went through all the reasons that I had come up with, and, as I said, we got along pretty well. Crist said, "Well, maybe that's it." I told him what I was going to do, which was to make sure that we didn't join up in that area, keep ships out of there for a period of time until we figured out what was going on. He said, "Well, okay. It's your call, do whatever you need to do, and you have them form up wherever you want them to form up, but don't go in there." I don't know that he necessarily agreed with me, but he didn't put any restrictions on me, and he didn't stand in the way. And it worked. That was a coup, in my opinion. I really believe that that was pretty neat, because my intel officer was beside himself with glee. He thought that was the greatest thing in the world.*

Paul Stillwell: With good reason.

Admiral Bernsen: With good reason, yes. It could have been another real nasty situation.

Paul Stillwell: How had they managed to lay those mines clandestinely? Because you did have ships in the area.

Admiral Bernsen: We didn't always have ships in there.

Paul Stillwell: I see.

Admiral Bernsen: We had them in there only when we were forming up the convoys. In the initial stages we were only forming up a convoy about every week, or whatever the time interval was. So we didn't have ships in there. The Iranians were using these rather innocuous-looking small civilian ships or dhows to go down there and do the mining. So they just picked a dark night, and they literally had had people down there, I'm sure, in dhows, in small boats. And they had had maps with them. They had American warships anchored, and they had put little X's on the map where they anchored. We're creatures of habit, and although I didn't anchor in Fujairah with *La Salle*, I went down there and visited ships anchored there. I suspect that one skipper probably said to the next skipper, "You know, we've got good holding ground right here, and this is the spot." And, hell, we were probably anchoring ships within 100 yards of each other for weeks. They weren't dumb. They could figure that out. So the Iranians went back to their intel guy and said, "Hey, here they are, where the X's are." Then they came down and put in a couple of rows of mines, not hard to do. We had gone in where we normally went. It would have been very, very unusual if we didn't.

---

* The Middle East Force staff intelligence officer was Commander Howell Conway Zeigler, USN.

Of course, shortly after that, as you well know, we sent the *Guadalcanal* down there to sweep the mines, and we got a whole bunch of countries involved. By that time we had other countries' minesweepers. The Brits were sweeping those mines, the Dutch got involved in sweeping those mines, I think. I'm not sure if the French did or not. But basically all those mines got swept. But it was a big operation, because we weren't sure. It was sort of an expanding search; they kept sweeping and sweeping. And the Brits and the Dutch found them. They were there. Then we ended up being able show the pattern.

Paul Stillwell: You alluded earlier to rules of engagement. Where did those originate for the Earnest Will operation?

Admiral Bernsen: That was all part of the op plan. When you write a plan for an operation of that type in today's day and age, why, rules of engagement are just another annex. And, of course, we had a very lengthy one. Rules of engagement, by the way, were approved all the way up through the Secretary of Defense. So while he may not have seen some parts of this plan, he certainly saw that part. The rules of engagement were really not very different from what we had been operating on all the time. And those rules had been laid down, basically, in 1979 and '80 when the Ayatollah had overthrown the Shah, and we—the Middle East Force—was in the area to begin with.[*] They were refined periodically as we went along. There were some changes made in '85, as I recall, when I was at CentCom. There were changes made that incorporated, for example, visit and search.

It was in the mid-'80s when we actually had an American merchant ship that was boarded by the Iranians, and that caused quite a flurry.[†] So then we changed the rules to accommodate those kinds of things, which never happened again, by the way, but if it had happened we would have rules to accommodate that. We put in a lot of rules because

---

[*] When the Shah left Iran in January 1979, the Ayatollah Ruhollah Khomeini seized power and declared the nation to be an Islamic republic. On 4 November 1979 Iranian militants seized the U.S. embassy in Teheran and took the staff members there as hostages. The hostages were ultimately released on 20 January 1981.
[†] On 12 January 1986 an Iranian rubber Zodiac boat pulled alongside the 600-foot-long U.S.-flag cargo ship *President Taylor*, which was in international waters en route Fujairah. A seven-man Iranian boarding party went aboard the American ship, performed an inspection to verify there was no contraband headed for Iraq, and then left. The inspection was in keeping with international law for a neutral ship in a war zone.

of the air wing that was flying off the aircraft carrier. This involved when they could shoot—the same with the surface ships. A whole host of rules were developed when the Iranians started shooting third-country neutral merchant ships. They would steam their little boats up alongside, and then they'd just fire rockets. I mean, it was absolutely ridiculous the kinds of things they did. So we generated some rules for that.

When they started flying helicopters, which was '85-'86, they mounted some missiles. The Iranians had some Italian missiles on those Italian helicopters. They weren't very effective, but we developed rules for interrogating helicopters from surface ships. How close they could comes before you were empowered to shoot them down, those kinds of things. So the rules of engagement were really developed on an ad hoc basis. There was a basic set of rules which were taken right out of the NATO lexicon, and I know national naval rules of engagement, little charts that we have, and they were added to.* It was an add-to process, an iterative process, and one that the national command authority was involved with at every step.

I wish I could remember. I think there were a couple of occasions when we actually made recommendations to change a rule. The request would go all the way up and down the chain. It was really something how when we needed a change right away, why, it would go quickly.

I think that's about enough on the mines and the mining. But I think it was very, very clear to me—and this has certainly proven to be true most recently in Desert Storm, that the best way to avoid mines is to prevent them from being laid. And that, while seemingly a very simple and straightforward statement, really is incredibly important, and it isn't always easy for people to grasp. Because, how do you do that? You do that by creating presence, a presence that is capable of surveilling.

You can surveil in a lot of ways. You can fly P-3 aircraft over an area constantly.† You could deploy small destroyers to cover an area. You can run smaller boats in an area, irregular intervals or constantly. Another way you can do it is to fly a lot of helicopters around. There were Iranians on these outlying islands, such as Farsi

---

* NATO – North Atlantic Treaty Organization.
† The Lockheed P-3 Orion is a high-performance land-based Navy patrol plane. It first entered operational squadrons in August 1962. The P-3C is 116 feet, 10 inches long; wingspan of 99 feet, 8 inches; gross weight of 135,000 pounds, and top speed of 473 miles per hour.

Island, which we were forbidden to attack. We couldn't bomb them down on the Abu Musa and those other islands in the lower Gulf. We weren't at war with these guys, so we couldn't go in. There was no rule of engagement that said we could go in indiscriminately and bomb the hell out of these guys. So here they had their little boats. We knew they had little boats. We had photographic intelligence, we had other kinds of intelligence that meant to me that in the middle of the night they could lay mines—the same thing they did off Farsi Island in the case of the *Bridgeton*—any other time.

Paul Stillwell: So you had to catch them in the act?

Admiral Bernsen: Right.

Paul Stillwell: Which is what you did with the *Iran Ajr*

Admiral Bernsen: And the only way you do that is by having somebody out there flying around. You may not be able to do it 24 hours a day, but you could do it at night, you can do it at irregular intervals, and you can do it in an overt enough manner that they know you're doing it, that they know that they are subject to attack, or surveillance, or whatever. If you look at the northern Gulf, starting at Farsi Island and going north, after the *Bridgeton*, and you recognize that the *Bridgeton* hit a mine and, if it hit a mine, there must be other mines there. Maybe there were mines all the way from Farsi Island to Kuwait, and I didn't have any way of knowing whether that was true or not.

The first instinct we had was, "Okay, we're going to regroup; we're going to get the two little—the ersatz minesweepers, I call them—and we're going to take that convoy up there."* We did that relatively quickly after the *Bridgeton*, as you know. It didn't take very long before we did that. And that was politically motivated. There were a lot of people who sure as hell didn't want to do that. But we hadn't done any real minesweeping. We were all just holding our breath. Well, they got there, and we continued to do the escort mission. But then the idea was, okay, we're going to go up

---

* The stopgap solution, the "ersatz minesweepers," involved the use of 150-foot-long commercial oilfield tugboats equipped with minesweeping cables flown from the United States. See page 29 above.

there, and we're going to sweep the mines. We knew the whole track to the west. We went up and swept the mines with the helicopters and also MSOs when they got there, and the other nations' minesweepers as well.* The next question was how were we going to prevent them from laying more mines.

Well, we didn't have MPA over there at the time; the P-3s came later.† We sure weren't going to take large destroyers and cruisers and run them up and down out there, because we didn't know whether they were going to hit another mine. So that wasn't feasible. So the only thing we had left, really, were the small boats and the helicopters. Well, the small boats, the only ones that the U.S. Navy has, are owned by the SEALs.‡ And that's when we decided to get the Mark III PBs over there.§ Well, Mark III PBs aren't very big; they really aren't. They're 65 feet long, a small crew, and they need a support base. Again, the first thing that you would think about was okay, fine, a port on the Saudi Coast, or maybe even Kuwait or Bahrain. But we were talking about going 40 miles, 50 miles offshore. It was just too far for them to go, particularly in bad weather. They'd beat themselves up. So we had to come up with another idea. And that's what gave birth to the famous barge business.

Paul Stillwell: Do you recall whose idea that was?

Admiral Bernsen: I really believe it was my idea. I've given some thought to that recently, and I really believe it was. Now, I'm not the guy that figured out how to execute it totally.

---

* MSOs were 1950s-era oceangoing minesweepers. Three each arrived in the Persian Gulf from the Atlantic and Pacific fleets after long journeys. Among them were the *Illusive* (MSO-448), *Inflict* (MSO-456), and *Fearless* (MSO-442), towed from the East Coast by the salvage ship *Grapple* (ARS-53). They departed Little Creek, Virginia, on 6 September 1987 and arrived in the Gulf of Oman on 2 November. The West Coast minesweepers that went to the Persian Gulf were the *Enhance* (MSO-437), *Conquest* (MSO-488), and *Esteem* (MSO-438).
† MPA – maritime patrol aircraft.
‡ SEALs are Navy personnel trained for sea, air, and land operations. In previous years similar individuals were designated as part of underwater demolition teams (UDTs). In addition to that specialty, the SEALs have a broader mission that includes commando-type operations ashore.
§ PB – patrol boat.

Paul Stillwell: Well, it was pretty vague to begin with: "We've got to have something as a base."

Admiral Bernsen: Sure. And we looked at a whole bunch of different things. I was up in Kuwait. I was talking to the head of the Kuwaiti Coast Guard, who had a couple of coast-wise boats with large helicopter platforms on the stern. Very, very nice boats that he offered to give me. And at that time we were just talking about putting some helicopters around the waters up near Kuwait. Again, we really hadn't developed this whole thought process here. I went down and looked at them. Each one had a helicopter platform, but the problem was that if you were going to meld the patrol boats with the helicopters, we were really talking about a whole bunch of boats. And that would involve a total of somewhere close to 200 people, and I think the accommodations on this little boat were 50 to 60 people max. So it really didn't lend itself. You could put some helicopters on it, though.

But I went back to *La Salle* and sat down and wrote it up. I don't honestly remember if I sent off the suggestion, the whole business, the concept, to George Crist or not. At some point I did, but I can't remember exactly when that point was. But what I did do was I wrote a paper, sat down with the staff, and talked about how we were going to go about doing this thing. Then I really did the rest of it myself, because we decided we needed to get something that would be large enough to support the helicopters and the patrol boats, basic patrol boats.

The most logical thing seemed to be some sort of a barge with a helicopter platform. There were all sorts of those all over the Gulf. The oil companies drilled for oil, and they had barges, and they had helicopters. I knew that, because I had been on some. In fact, I had been on some back in '80, in Bahrain. So I called a friend of mine in Houston who owned a small company called Inter-Marine. It provides oil service craft to the oil industry all over the world, primarily in the Persian Gulf, as well as in Indonesia. I went out on a limb a little bit, because I told my Texas friend about my plan on the non-secure phone in vague terms. I didn't tell him what I wanted these things for, but I think he understood what I wanted. I said, "Basically, what I'm looking for are some barges that would accommodate 100-200 people on board, that have a helicopter capability, and do you have any idea who might have some of these?" He said he'd get back to me. I said, "Make it pretty quick." I had a call back within 12 hours. He gave me the names of three different companies; one of them had an agent in Bahrain.

Paul Stillwell: Did you feel you had a blank checkbook on something like this?

Admiral Bernsen: I didn't know what I had at this point in time, other than I had received an assurance from the head of the Kuwaiti Oil Tanker Company. He didn't really understand what it was I was doing, but I had impressed upon him the fact that I thought it was very important, and it had to do with protecting his ships, and that made it important. He had told me that if the Kuwaiti Coast Guard ships didn't suit me, and I could find something else that suited me—that if I could find some other barges, as I termed them, and I couldn't figure out an Arab name for things like that, so that was a good compromise—that he would figure out how to pay for them. So, no, I didn't know that I had a blank check, but I knew I had something in the bank somewhere.

I was ashore at this time in Bahrain in the administrative offices, and I had ready access to a phone. After receiving the names of the barge owners from my friend, I literally locked myself in my office, and I just started making phone calls around the Gulf. I talked to a number of people, several of whom I had met before, so it wasn't totally strange, and found that one these companies did have a barge. Yes, it was in Abu Dhabi, and it wasn't in very good shape. A second company had a couple of barges, one of which was in Singapore. They would be happy to make it available, but it was going to take two weeks to tow it to the Gulf.

Then I finally called the third outfit, which I probably should have done first. It was Brown & Root, the company that has an office in Bahrain. I've known people in Brown & Root for many years. There was a British fellow in charge. Brown & Root, back in 1980 when oil drilling was very active in the Gulf, had some 1,000 people in Bahrain. In 1987, they had 50, so the operation had gotten much, much smaller. Commensurate with that, back in 1980 they had a whole bunch of barges that they were using, of one kind or another. Two of them were tied up in Bahrain. So right there, under my very nose, literally not a mile away over on the other side of the port, were the

Wimbrown and *Hercules*—right there. John Rex was the fellow's name. He came over to my office that afternoon. We had an opportunity to talk, and, again, I had to couch this in relatively broad terms, but I think John basically knew what I wanted.

Paul Stillwell: Was he a local Brown & Root representative?

Admiral Bernsen: He was the Brown & Root supervisor in Bahrain. I had checked on him, and I knew that he was quite reliable and would be very discreet. I had done that checking through—again, through my shipping contact in Texas, through the head of Brown & Root, the president of Brown & Root, who was never officially in any of these negotiations. But it was my understanding that he would do anything that the United States Navy wanted, within reason, that he would provide full support. So there had been some phone communication between Brown & Root and my friend even before I called, or at least about the same time. Within 24 hours, Mr. Rex and his assistant had a set of drawings on my desk in Bahrain, showing me both of the barges, showing me exactly how the decks and the compartments were laid out, where people would berth, and all the rest of it. After studying those plans, we then got in my automobile and drove over to the local port. We found the pier where the two barges were located and went aboard. I was convinced almost immediately that they were exactly what I was looking for.

My problem at this point was basically how to get them working for me. That turned out not to be very hard. I went back to my office, called Kuwait, got ahold of Abdullah Fatah, who was the head of KOTC, actually got ahold of his British assistant, who was a pretty good friend of mine, told him I'd found two barges and that I had a ballpark number on how much they would cost. As I recall, Brown & Root was offering a six-month lease. The basic lease was around a million bucks for the two of them. That included the manpower to run them, the cooks, and everybody else. Additional funds would be required to upgrade them, in particular to rehab the helicopter pad.

Paul Stillwell: What kind of shape were they in?

Admiral Bernsen: Actually, they were in pretty good shape. *Hercules*, I don't think, had been to sea for about a year. They weren't in bad shape, but they did need some cleaning up. The response at the other end was a very reasonable one. Mr. Rex was on an airplane that night from Bahrain to Kuwait with a contract. He came back the next day with the contract signed, and in essence we had a handshake all around, and the Kuwaiti Oil Tanker Company committed to that million dollars renting two barges for six months.

My problem at this time was that I had run out of people. We had so many balls in the air on the staff because of the planning and running all of the tanker escort missions, all the liaison with the Kuwaitis, and the fact that our force of ships had grown, doubled literally, within a matter of a couple of months. By this time now we had minesweepers that had come our way, we had the small patrol boats that had arrived, which is another story entirely. They were brought in through Saudi Arabia under great, great cover in C-5 airplanes with all the SEALs and all the rest of these guys. They were all sitting in the middle of Manama, Bahrain, and my small staff had only one or two guys extra by that time. I had a few mine countermeasure folks that were add-ons, and I had some SEALs a couple of guys who were add-ons. But, in essence, the basic staff hadn't changed any, and I didn't have anybody else to do any of these things. I was down to lieutenant jaygees and lieutenants who were doing things that normally captains and commanders would do.[*]

A very fortuitous thing happened at this point. An absolutely marvelous naval officer by the name of Frank Lugo showed up on the scene, compliments of OP-06.[†] He had just left a job as operations officer on the Second Fleet staff, where he had worked for Admiral Hank Mustin.[‡] He was between jobs. Mustin had called Crist on the phone and asked him if maybe I needed some help, and offered Lugo to come out as my chief of staff. Well, I already had a chief of staff. I didn't need a deputy or chief of staff. But as a special projects guy, I mean, he was manna from heaven.

Frank Lugo was one of the most energetic, smart, dynamic guys in the United States Navy, as far as I'm concerned. I've known him for a long time. Anyway, he got two jobs from me. One of them was to put those barges into commission. I gave him a

---
[*] Jaygee – lieutenant (junior grade).
[†] Captain Frank J. Lugo, USN, arrived in Bahrain on 12 August 1987.
[‡] Vice Admiral Henry C. Mustin, USN, commanded the Second Fleet, September 1984 to September 1986.

SEAL and a Marine officer to help him, and he did it. He planned it, supervised it, worked with the Brown & Root guys to install defensive positions on the barges, to improve the helicopter platforms, all of the changes that had to be made to make the platforms fit Navy helicopter specs, everything from fire extinguishers to special lighting. Then came the real hard part. Quite frankly, in retrospect, up until now it just sort of moved ahead very quickly, literally within a week to two weeks. I can't remember exactly, but it went very quickly from conception to a basic plan to hiring the barges.

By the next time I went over to the pier, literally a week after the lease had been signed, there were 250 workers climbing all over these things: painting and cleaning and washing and scrubbing and bringing food aboard, and the whole business. But, unfortunately, there were a lot of people in Navy who thought this was a cockamamie idea. In fact, it wasn't just the Navy; it was the Marines. Interestingly enough, I'm not too sure what the hell the Marines had to do with this, since there weren't going to be any Marines on those things. But there was an unfortunate attempt—unfortunate from my point of view at least—to equate one of these barges with the barracks in Beirut.[*] There was a very significant group of people in the United States Navy at very high levels, as well as at other levels, who really believed that putting a barge up in the northern Gulf with PBs and helicopters and whatever else on it was simply giving the Iranians a target. And, depending on the context, I could understand that point of view.

My problem was that the alternatives were so much worse. The alternatives being if we did not put some consistent surveillance platform into the northern Gulf, I was absolutely convinced, and I think for good reason, that the Iranians would lay more mines, and the next time it was going to be a U.S. warship that was going to be hit. We were not only going to suffer massive loss of life, but that, in essence, the American public and the Congress were going to say, "That's enough of that nonsense. Either get out, or we're going to go to war." Neither alternative was a good alternative.

I felt that the Iranian air threat, and that was really the only way they were going to get at the barges, was minimal. We had had a situation—again, you have to take it in context—two years before where two Iranian aircraft had strayed across the Gulf and

---

[*] On 23 October 1983, a suicide terrorist drove a truck filled with the equivalent of 12,000 pounds of explosives into the Marine Corps barracks in Beirut, Lebanon. The resulting explosion killed 241 Americans and wounded 70.

been shot down by the Saudis, assisted by the U.S. Air Force AWACS.* I personally felt that that incident had made a great impression on the Iranians, and they weren't really in the business of flying their own airplanes around the Gulf. I felt that we could put tugs permanently assigned—and the Kuwaitis agreed to pay for that too—alongside the barges, and every two days we'd move them to a different location. I did not believe that the Iranians had satellite capability. I didn't believe that they had good enough intelligence of any other kind to pinpoint those barges, particularly if we kept moving them around.

Then, as far as surface-to-surface action was concerned, we had more than enough capability in the form of the patrol boats and the armed helicopters to attack and defeat any Iranians that might come around. It was just totally, totally unrealistic that the Iranians were going to steam one of their frigates from Bandar Abbas all the way up in the northern Gulf and take one of these barges under fire. I mean, that wasn't going to happen; that wasn't part of it. So that in my view the argument against deploying the barges was more emotional than anything else. It was not really based on any rational analysis, but it was emotional, based on the assumption that something like what happened in Beirut could happen here. I just felt that the actual context in fear was totally different. The threat was different and really not very much of a threat, and that we just simply had much more capability to avoid a Beirut kind of an incident, but that we didn't have the capability to surveil without the barges.

Paul Stillwell: And the sea gave you a kind of moat around those barges that you didn't have in the Beirut situation.

Admiral Bernsen: All sorts of islands and all kinds of cover up in that area of the Gulf: oil rigs, and islands, and all kinds of business. And although the Saudis hadn't given us permission to bring them into Saudi waters at that time, which they later did, I really believed that we could skirt along the edge and close enough to the western Gulf that the Iranians simply wouldn't dare come into that area.

---

* AWACS – airborne warning and control system. This is an aerial look-down radar and tracking system carried on board the Air Force's E-3 Sentry, a modified Boeing 707 airliner with a rotating radome on top.

The initial arguments in support of the barge concept had been received very favorably by none other than the Chairman. He had gotten a copy of my paper and had written a message to George Crist strongly supporting the concept and suggesting that I move forward very quickly. And that's what I did. Well, we were going to put some armament on those barges, some .50-caliber weapons and a few other odds and ends. About three and a half weeks after the inception date, I figured that we were probably a week, week and a half away from deploying these things. We had all the folks ready to get on board and go.

Then General Crist showed up with an entourage of all kinds of people. They were mostly from the naval systems commands, various other offices, and his own staff. I welcomed him with open arms. We immediately went down to the barges, and we made a full tour. Quite frankly, I was very impressed with the progress that was being made and was convinced that he was impressed too. Nothing could have been further from the truth.

Frankly, it was probably our most unpleasant afternoon. I'm not sure how to characterize it, but he frankly was ballistic over the whole thing. After the tour, he was very strident: "How are we going to defend this? We're crazy, we're not going to do it with the .50 caliber, and this is ridiculous. They're going to blow us out of the water. We need three-quarter-inch steel plating. We need to put up sandbags; we need DIVAD; we need all kinds of defenses. We need a complete communications van and suite."[*] I mean, it went on and on and on. I just stood there in utter disbelief, because while all of these things might be nice to have, I was convinced that even with all of the tremendous support we were getting out of that small shipyard, we were talking about months, literally months. And in the meantime we were going to have a mine strike. But there wasn't any gainsaying it. I mean, it was going to be all that, or we weren't going to deploy.

For a few minutes I actually thought, "Well, maybe it isn't worth it. Maybe it just isn't worth the effort. I'm not going to ever do it." I almost had the feeling that even if we did everything that he said, there would still be something undone. In other words, the next visit would be another 52 requirements, and we would go on from there. In

---

[*] DIVAD – The Army's M247 Sergeant York division air defense system.

retrospect, and subsequently, I found out that it was really the Navy that had put the press on Crist. He had convened a small conference down in CentCom. Admiral Baggett, who was CinCLant at the time, had sent his emissary—interestingly enough, a good friend of mine—down to CentCom and argued that my plan was a bummer.*

Paul Stillwell: Was this more of the Beirut mentality?

Admiral Bernsen: Absolutely, absolutely. The assertion was that the barges were not defensible. The Navy's position was, "we're in the business of sailing ships, not barges. This is crazy, it's ersatz, it doesn't make any sense. It smacks of Indian wars or something. It's so farfetched and so out of context of a Navy thing. And here we're talking about, you know, a galley crew of 50 Indians and Filipinos with no clearances. How do you protect the guys in the barge? I mean, they're going to come in and stab us to death in the middle of the night." I mean, the arguments were legion. I mean, it was just, "Bernsen's gone out of his tree. He's got this crazy idea; he's continuing to move ahead. He's got the Chairman to back him up, but in actual fact it's insanity. The Iranians are going to get him, and if they don't get him, the terrorists are going to infiltrate, and they're going to kill everybody. It's just going to be plumb crazy."

Paul Stillwell: Did you have any self-doubts at that point?

Admiral Bernsen: I really didn't. I truly didn't, and I think I can absolutely and honestly state that. All that I did was get mad. I got absolutely furious. I had sent Lugo, the barge architect and my principal number-one guy—I had sent him to the meeting. I am convinced, in retrospect, and I wish Frank were here today, that if Frank had not gone and argued as effectively as he did, that the end result would have been the scuttling of the barges at that meeting. That would have been it, and Crist would not have come over and told me to beef up the defenses. He would have gotten a message that said, "That's it, forget it. Turn them back over to the Bahrainis. We'll go on and do something else."

---

* Admiral Lee Baggett, Jr., USN, served as Supreme Allied Commander Atlantic and Commander in Chief Atlantic Command from 27 November 1985 to 22 November 1988.

But I think Frank went back, with the charts, showed where we were going to deploy, described how we were going to move these things frequently, how we were going to put them all the way to the west, and then as we cleared the area we would slowly move them out into the shipping lanes a little further east.

All of the conservative plans that we had, how the PBs would be tied in, how they would deploy and patrol, the support that the helicopters would provide, the synergism involved here, the fact that we were going to put a combatant with a good effective radar as far north as we could in unmined waters, so that there would be that kind of radar coverage so we would be able to see an Iranian aircraft. Then we would have a tie-in with the AWACS. And he went on and on and on. I think he was damn convincing. We had gone over his pitch before he left. I picked him on purpose, because he had a lot of credibility, and he had become absolutely convinced that this was the way to go.

Paul Stillwell: Well, he was a blue-suiter too; that helped.

Admiral Bernsen: A blue-suiter, he was absolutely convincing. And he had gotten so involved in putting these things together. Every day he would come back to the flagship, and he'd say, "This is terrific; this is the way it's going to be. This is a great idea, and we're going to move this thing." For the SEALs, this was exactly their piece of meat. They loved it. With all the secret cover and everything, it was like a great big game to them.

Paul Stillwell: And the boat units too.

Admiral Bernsen: Oh yes, and the boat units—what they did on the barges. They put all sorts of rubberized padding around the barges so these guys could tie up. They put davits on them, and we had huge cranes that were integral to both of the barges. They could pick the boats right up and put them in cradles on the thing when the weather got bad. I mean, it was a piece of cake; it was stupendous.

Well, Lugo came back, and he was really upset. He said, "Boss, "they're going to kill us."

I said, "Well, what's the problem?"

He said, "Nobody wants us." He had with him a two-page message that had been written by a Marine general out at CinCPac. In fact, he was the J-3 at CinCPac.* It was a two-page diatribe about what an incredibly bad idea this was. Well, Crist bent to the pressure and came out with all of these directives: "You know, we're going to make this thing impregnable." And he used the term "Khe Sanh" himself.† That's what we were going to construct here. We were going to construct a barge that was able to withstand the attacks like at Khe Sanh. But at least he backed me up.

I don't want to be unkind to General Crist, but I think the fact that Crowe also was on board stiffened Crist a little bit. I sat down with him and said, "You know, really you've made this very hard for us."

He said, "Hal, you either do all of these things I'm telling you to do, or there isn't going to be any barge. There won't be any surveillance platform up in the northern Gulf, and we're just going to have to go ahead in a conventional way and whatever."

Well, when he put it like that, I said, "Okay, so we'll continue." And we did. As I predicted, it took weeks. But by September we were ready to go. We put a complete complement of SEALs and boats and helicopters and everything on the *Hercules*, and we moved her out for a two-day test period, and right behind her was the *WimBrown*. We ended up moving *Hercules* northeast of Bahrain, operating the helicopters and all the rest of it, and it was working pretty well. We put *Wimbrown* just to the east of Bahrain, in the Bahraini ship channel, just outside of it, and started operating her.

That was when Joint Task Force Middle East was born.‡ Probably the individual who was absolutely, completely, and totally dedicated to scuttling the whole program was Admiral Brooks. He thought this was absolutely, totally wrong. And there ensued a period of intense struggle. Just before Brooks arrived on the scene, Crist had authorized me to deploy *Hercules*. We were literally in the process of towing her up to her eventual

---

* Major General Royal Moore Jr., USMC, was operations officer for Pacific Command.
† Khe Sanh, South Vietnam, was the site of a Marine Corps base during combat operations between January and July 1968.
‡ The new command was formed 10 September 1987. The first individual to hold the command was Rear Admiral Dennis M. Brooks, USN, a naval aviator who was senior to Admiral Bernsen. Brooks's flagship was the cruiser *Long Beach* (CGN-9), which remained outside the Persian Gulf.

location when JTFME came on the scene, found out she was being towed up there and ordered me to stop. I mean, it was crazy, and we ended up with a real tug of war.

I think what finally got it unscrewed was that the Chairman wanted to know what the hell was going on, and why wasn't *Hercules* deployed. And basically we were forced to tell him that we had been told not to do that. So that order was countermanded, and I can't give you the date. I don't remember exactly the time, but it was mid-October sometime. *Hercules* did deploy. She deployed up north, and *Wimbrown* deployed sometime after.[*] In retrospect, I think they were very successful. The Iranians, to the best of my knowledge, had not deployed any mines between the time of the *Bridgeton* and the night in October when the small helicopters flying off of *Hercules* came upon—in the ship channel—a couple of Iranian Boghammars, or one Boghammar and a dhow.[†] The helos were taken under fire with what we later figured was a Stinger, the small shoulder-held surface-to-air missile that we gave the Afghani. The helicopters, again, were working under the rules of engagement as they existed, that is, if you're fired on you can return fire, and they sank the Boghammar. The Boghammar was later recovered out of 100-plus feet of water and displayed on board *Hercules*. I've got a whole flock of pictures of it. The helicopter guys did a hell of a job on that ship—the boat shot full of holes. And we found in the boat the box in which the Stinger missile had come, which proved that indeed it was a Stinger missile that the Iranians had fired.

I think that, again, was a pretty significant turning point, because it essentially took away the night from the Iranians. After that they rarely ventured off Farsi Island. We just didn't see those little boats running around out there shooting at people. They were really frightened, because they were aware that we had the capability to kill them and were willing to do that as well. We also had the will to do that.

From that point till the end of the war, there were no mines dropped in the northern Gulf. The *Roberts*, which was struck the next spring, was hit in the central Gulf, further to the south. Interestingly enough, in an area which in the fall of 1987, November of '87 in particular, I recommended to CinCCent that we station an LPH equipped with Marine and Navy helicopters to form, in essence, another barge, an actual Navy ship, host

---

[*] The *Hercules* deployed in October 1987 and the *Wimbrown* in November.
[†] Boghammar is a type of high-speed coastal patrol boat. These attacks took place the night of 8 October 1987 as AH-6 Seabat helicopters retaliated against the Iranian boats.

platform. Admiral Brooks rejected that as being a very, very bad idea. And unfortunately in that case he carried the day. You know, it's hard to be really positive about those things in retrospect, but I suspect there's a very good chance that had we done that—literally, it was another ship, more assets, more forces—but had we done that, the Iranians would never have been able to put the mines in the central Gulf, and *Roberts* would have never been mined.

If I might digress for just a second, something that I think is really important here is that during Desert Shield we, the Navy, were prevented from venturing into the northern Gulf, north of 27-30, to surveil and monitor minelaying during the six months prior to the war—prior to Desert Storm.* If we had been allowed to do that, and had mounted an effective surveillance effort—I'm not suggesting barges, but just Navy ships, helicopters, and we had more than enough assets to do that, remember it wouldn't have been a *Tripoli*, we wouldn't have hit a mine, because they never would have laid mines.† I think if there was one great mistake that was made, by the NCA really, I think it was a political decision more than anything else, that was it.‡ Fortunately, it didn't cost us a great deal of life, but it cost us two ships.

Paul Stillwell: After all the hassles you went through to get those on station, it must have been very satisfying to achieve that.

Admiral Bernsen: Well, it was. It was incredibly satisfying, and the amazing thing is that the night of the Boghammar incident was either the first or the second night operation off the *Hercules*. So it was literally right after all this nonsense of finally getting her up there, and she went out, and those guys did their jobs, literally right away. That was, I must say, very satisfying and probably was—again, it's hard to conjecture, but it tended to silence JTFME, even though he still didn't like it. And he believed firmly that the helicopter pilots had operated contrary to the ROE. He thought that we had been

---

* This is a reference to 27 degrees, 30 minutes north latitude.
† At 0345 on the morning of 18 January 1991, after operating for 11 hours in an undetected Iraqi minefield, the amphibious assault ship *Tripoli* (LPH-10) hit a moored Iraqi contact mine. The resulting explosion ripped a 16- by 20-foot hole below the ship's waterline.
‡ NCA – national command authority.

much too provocative, that if the helicopters hadn't flown over the Boghammar, the Boghammar wouldn't have shot at him. I'm not sure I can understand that line of thought or reason, but at any rate the barges stayed up there and became, of course, fixtures for the rest of the conflict.

Paul Stillwell: They became a deterrent.

Admiral Bernsen: I hope they did. I think they did. I really believe that they had a very important and effective role to play and that, in hindsight, they were also very cheap. The Kuwaitis continued to pay the bill. They paid Brown & Root for *all* of the incredible defensive enhancements that we put on those barges. They paid for all the steel work, the hangars, the helicopter deck improvements, the sandbags, the whole nine yards. The only thing the U.S. Government paid for, to the best of my knowledge, were those things that were unique to the military, such as communications equipment and the weapons themselves that were put on board the barges.

Of course, the fact is they were never attacked. There was no terrorist insertion or infiltration of the mess decks or anything else, and the food wasn't bad either. Can you translate this to someplace else in some other conflict? I think you'd have to be very careful. On the other hand, we are now actively talking to the Navy about mine countermeasures mother ships as being something in POM 94 perhaps.* We have talked seriously about using jack-up rigs towed by, or actually placed on semi-submersibles that steam at 14 knots to some area, some region, where you want to set up a floating base—but you don't want to use a ship—that could support helicopters, small-boat ops, and that sort of thing. So I think it's another arrow in the quiver, so to speak. It's another option, and I'm so glad that I was a part of it. It was fun.

Paul Stillwell: Did any of the add-ons that General Crist mandated prove useful, in your view?

---

* POM – program objectives memorandum, an element of the budgeting process. This refers to the budget for fiscal year 1994.

Admiral Bernsen: In retrospect, the add-ons that he mandated were all prudent. My problem at the time was—

Paul Stillwell: Time.

Admiral Bernsen: Time, exactly. The Chairman kept saying, "When are you guys going to get surveillance up there? When are the helicopters going to be flying in the northern Gulf?" And you cannot add tons of three-quarter-inch steel and new hangars and all of these things overnight. We're talking about building these all from scratch with Indian/Filipino labor, with a few British supervisors. It did take time, and we had to bring the 25-millimeter chain guns from the States and construct platforms on which to put them that were sufficiently sturdy that they could be screwed in, the whole bit. It was a monumental task. It would have been a monumental task for Newport News shipyard, I swear, just because of the ad hoc nature of it. So it took time. That was my only complaint. Once they got up there, and they had all this stuff on board, we all felt much better about it. Certainly the guys on board felt more secure. They had all these weapons and sandbags and all the rest of it. It was terrific.

In retrospect, I really believe that if you were using the patrol boats and the helicopters as forward defense, defense in depth, whatever you want to call it, that that in essence was sufficient. And that was the original plan. The plan was not to make the barges impregnable. The plan was to simply make them bases from which you could operate effectively. They were meant to be like an aircraft carrier. An aircraft carrier was never designed to be impregnable. The air wing is what keeps her safe basically. That was the idea.

Paul Stillwell: Well, I remember the combatant ships got beefed up. You mentioned the chain guns. They were put on cruisers, for example. Where was that effort supervised?

Admiral Bernsen: It's extremely hard to pinpoint where the idea came from or who thought of that. Those things were discussed through Navy channels. We knew that we needed some sort of a weapon that was effective against small boats. It had been discussed even before I got out there. But once we were in the escort business—lots more ships, more attention, the *Bridgeton* mining, now maybe they were going to come get us. Now it became a lot more intense. I think once it got back through Navy channels, through the type commander, fleet, and then up to OpNav and systems commands, we had a bunch of engineers and a whole bunch of other people. You get literally so many people involved that it's very difficult to figure out who came up with the idea that, hey, the 25-millimeter Bushmaster is the best answer to the small-gun problem. We obviously needed something a little bit bigger than a .50-caliber. What's available? That was available in the system, so we were able to install those.

The installation was done back in the States before the ships left, although we did a few in the Gulf. Ships that had already come over didn't have any weapons on board, so they actually sent some 25-millimeter guns over to the Gulf and installed them over there, using tiger teams as well as some minor shipyard assistance. There were many different ways of doing that sort of business.

A couple of things that we did do, however, which I think are worth noting. My staff didn't have a CNA rep, and I didn't have a NASAP rep, NASAP being a naval science advisory program.[*] NASAP reps are located at the fleet CinC and the component commander level. Interestingly enough, NavCent, the one-star in Hawaii, is a Navy component commander. He had a NASAP representative who didn't do anything or very little according to Admiral Jesberg.[†] He called me up one day and said, "I got this guy here who's not really being usefully employed. Could you use him?"

I said, "I don't even know what he is. What's NASAP?" So he tried to explain that to me, and I said, "Look, I can use any man I get. If the guy is bright, imaginative, and can think, maybe he can contribute." Well, it turned out the guy was terrific.

Paul Stillwell: Who was he? Do you remember his name?

---

[*] CNA – Center for Naval Analyses.
[†] Rear Admiral Ronald H. Jesberg, USN, Commander Naval Forces Central Command.

Admiral Bernsen: Dave Dittmer was the guy from CNA, and the other guy I can't remember, honestly.* I got his name written down—and I've run into him since. But he came over there, and basically he was perfect for us, because his connection was with the science community and the development community in the Navy. So if you had an idea, and you were going to build a prototype of something, he could figure out which scientists or think tank or NRL or whoever could build it for us.† Well, I mean, talk about an ad hoc operation. What I needed was exactly what I got. He helped a little bit on a few design features on the barges, but most of that was done by the time he got there. He did do some excellent follow-on work. For example, there was the issue of how to decoy Silkworm missiles. This guy got the group over from NRL and designed the decoys that were eventually purchased by the Kuwaiti Government and stuck in the Kuwaiti harbor that decoyed the Silkworms after they had that first initial success up there and hit the U.S.-flag ship.

Paul Stillwell: *Sea Isle City*.‡

Admiral Bernsen: That's right. And subsequent to that, we deployed a whole bunch of these tetrahedrons, whatever the hell they were, all over the port up there, and it was this guy that made that all happen. Everybody in the Gulf during the summer of '87 was going crazy with the heat, and he was instrumental in getting this vest designed. You put ice packs in a vest so the guys could go down in the engine room and not fry. Night vision devices, some laser devices that we were going to use, some optical devices that we were going to use on the bridge for targeting, for example, those chain guns. The business about looking for mines with lasers and various other optical devices.

Now, I'm not saying that he invented all these things. What I'm suggesting is that he would run around and say, "What's the problem? What do you need?"

---

* David L. Dittmer was a senior analyst and field representative for the Center for Naval Analyses from 1973 to 2011.
† NRL – Naval Research Laboratory.
‡ On 16 October 1987 the re-flagged tanker *Sea Isle City* was at the Al-Ahmadi terminal in Kuwait when she was hit by an Iranian Silkworm missile. The ship's master, Captain John J. Hunt, was blinded by the explosion. The missile did extensive damage to the tanker.

Guys would say, "Well, you know, that's what we need. Or we need this. Everybody's getting hot; we need one of those." Then he'd sit down, and he'd write up a paragraph or so on what the problem was, and he'd start firing messages out, and I just gave him carte blanche. He could send messages to anybody he wanted to. But he was sending messages to all of these odd places I'd never heard of before. You know, "Dear Joe, this is our problem. Do you think you can help me?" The next day, people would show up out of the blue, and they were buddies of his that came from the community. They'd go out and look around, and they'd draw things and go back and create stuff. That was terrific.

I didn't have time, nor did the staff have time, to really get involved in very much of that. I mean, he had to be a self-starter, and we had lots of those kinds of people. That's what was sort of neat about it. He would come in, and I gave him 15 projects the day he showed up, after he described to me what he was all about. I just went down a whole bunch of things that I had scribbled down in my notes that I probably was never going to be able to do anything about. He said, "Yes, sir." And he took his list of 15 items, and things started to happen. It was terrific. I wouldn't have known whom to call.

Paul Stillwell: Ideal, as you say.

Admiral Bernsen: For that crazy situation we had over there. The CNA rep was extremely valuable because of his analytical mode. I mean, if you had X number of mines in the water and X number of yards, or a square mile, and he could figure out what the chances were that you were going to hit one of them, those kinds of things. Well, that's really not all that ludicrous, because, actually, numbers of escorts and how many times should you go through that particular route before you change the route, and what are the probabilities? I mean, he did all kinds of things like that which were very helpful to us, plus a whole bunch of other stuff. But it was that kind of analysis that we needed.

Paul Stillwell: You had a great, great logistic buildup with all of this. How did you handle that on the staff?

Admiral Bernsen: Well, I had a lieutenant commander logistics officer; he was a terrific guy. But the main logistics depot, if you will, or transshipment point, was, of course, Bahrain. Bahrain had a lieutenant who worked for the CO of the administrative support unit—again, a good guy, but the minute we ended up with doubling the number of ships and then the minesweeps and the SEALs, etc., etc., we ended up with ASU being literally overrun. I mean, the packing cases filled up the streets, and the pathways, and the warehouses were chockablock. We had stuff all over the parking apron out at the airport at Bahrain. It rapidly got totally out of hand, not to mention the mail problem. It was just crazy.

A fellow who immediately recognized from afar that we had a serious problem was NavSup.

Paul Stillwell: Admiral Walker?

Admiral Bernsen: Yes, exactly, Ted Walker.[*] And I had a couple of talks with him subsequent to getting back in '88. In fact, I came up to Washington specifically to thank him for all his support. He went to the CNO and told the CNO straight up that he thought we needed all sorts of help, and we weren't getting any. Well, I don't think Admiral Trost was that anxious to send us a whole bunch of extra help in the way of administrative support ashore.[†] And there were a whole bunch of reasons for that—probably most of this he knows better than I do.

But Ted, bless his soul, the first guy he sent was a captain. This guy literally walked aboard and said, "What do you need? I'm here to help, and I'll set up logistics ashore and do whatever I can." And that's what he did. He sat down, surveyed the situation, figured out the best way in which to support the organization, came up with a list of manning personnel, cargo-handling groups, all kinds of people that are necessary that I certainly had no idea about.

---

[*] Rear Admiral Edward K. Walker Jr., SC, USN, Commander Naval Supply Systems Command and Chief of the Supply Corps.
[†] Admiral Carlisle A. H. Trost, USN, was Chief of Naval Operations from 1 July 1986 to 29 June 1990.

The other key thing was that we needed more space. Actually, I went to our ambassador, Sam Zakhem, and said, "We've got to have some space."* Between the two of us, with a little help from a couple other folks, we managed to get a whole bunch of warehouses that were unused; they were long idle down near the pier area in Manama. They were not leased from the Bahraini Government but from a private company. We went through the Bahraini Government to get it done. It was another one of these strange handshake deals initially.

We were able to do that, and I remember the day that the ambassador and I went to see the Foreign Minister. He sat down, and the ambassador said, "Hal, you tell the Foreign Minister what it is you need." And I laid out the problem. The Foreign Minister said he was sure that we could arrange something. We ended up getting, I think it was three warehouses, and then we went into a long-term negotiation for another warehouse at the airport. During my tenure there, we were unable to come to terms on the airport deal, and I'm not sure the reason why. But we did get the big warehouses on the pier.

We got a whole bunch of additional folks that Walker sent out, enlisted guys, who actually were working the storage. The way it all worked out is we had at least three major MAC flights a day that would come in at the airport.† We had a very energetic Filipino contract bunch that would unload all this stuff. We would then truck it across town, store it in the warehouses, catalogue it, make sure that the parts that needed to get out in a hurry were separated. They were actually kept at the airport for the most part and then ferried out to the ships by helicopter. The other stuff would be at the port; ships would come in periodically, once a week or so, and we'd lighter the stuff out using contract lighterage or put the ship alongside the pier. But most of them were out in the stream and anchored.

As we went along, the supply effort grew larger and larger, and we ended up using Fujairah. We would bring commercial shipping or MSC shipping in from the Philippines to Fujairah.‡ We'd actually break the material down on the pier, and then we

---

* Dr. Sam Zakhem was U.S. ambassador to Bahrain from 1986 to 1989.
† MAC – Military Airlift Command, an element of the U.S. Air Force.
‡ MSC – the Military Sealift Command operates a number of government-owned ships crewed by civil service mariners and at times augments these with charters of privately-owned vessels.

would bring in an AFS.* He would take the material aboard and store it properly. Then he would come into the Gulf and act as a standard stores ship and transfer supplies to the ships not only in the Gulf but out in the battle group as well. So it became a pretty sophisticated operation, and it worked very well. If it hadn't been for Ted Walker and his guys and the way they really pressed the issue, again, I think I would have been very hard pressed to do this, because I had a lieutenant commander who was up to his ears in alligators just handling the things that he could handle. And this lieutenant at ASU, when the 500 boxes arrived and inundated his little three-acre place there, he was overwhelmed. So we ended up putting quite a few supply folks on the beach.

But, all in all, when you think about it, not very many. I mean, when I say quite a few, I'm talking about 25 or 30 guys. So we're really not talking about very many people. There were lots of folks in Bahrain who were looking for work. Lots of little companies were more than happy to go out and hire Indians and Filipinos and all the rest. There weren't many Bahrainis who were working, but all of those third-country nationals with the turbans and the ragged shorts that exist in Bahrain and do those kinds of things; they had jobs. There were plenty of them. They worked hard 12 hours a day for very little.

Paul Stillwell: One thing that impressed me was all the canned soda on board the *White Plains*, so that seemed to be a high-demand commodity.†

Admiral Bernsen: Outside of the barges, the most interesting issue for me and the most satisfying—and I think I'll probably end up this now, at least at this point—was the free fuel contract. That is a fascinating one, and I think I remember the circumstances pretty well. I must admit I do not have the exact dates down. I'm going to go back and research because I want to get the dates.

It was during one of a number of trips to Kuwait in June, when we went through the final stages with the Kuwaitis regarding how these ships were going to be escorted and handled. When Admiral Crowe and I had were there earlier in May, as we were

---
* AFS was the designation for a Navy combat stores ship.
† USS *White Plains* (AFS-4) was a combat stores ship that replenished Navy ships in both the Persian Gulf and the North Arabian Sea.

walking from the Emir's office over to see the Prime Minister, I had talked to him in the courtyard. I told him my take, from meetings that I had had already with the Kuwaiti Oil Tanker Company and the Kuwaiti Oil Minister, was that we might be able to get some free fuel from them. If nothing else, at the northern end of the convoy escorts, they could certainly bring some barges out to put some gas in our ships. As a result of the conversation, Admiral Crowe raised the issue specifically with the Prime Minister. And the Prime Minister said, "Oh, yes, be certain we will provide fuel."

Well, that was really fortuitous, because it was Crowe's statement and the Prime Minister's response, which was in the affirmative, which I used later on as an entering point for other discussions with senior Kuwaiti officials. I was able to say, "Yes, but your Prime Minister said we could get some gas." What the Prime Minister didn't say was how much gas, and I don't think the Prime Minister had the foggiest idea of what I was talking about later on. But, at any rate, in June, during a conversation with the Kuwaiti Oil Tanker Company CEO, Al Fatah, I mentioned that the escort operation was costing us a hell of a lot in fuel, and that small amount we were getting in barges at the northern end of the trip really didn't amount to a great deal. And that, "Your Prime Minister did say, and I thought really we ought to get more fuel if at all possible."

He picked it up, and he said, "Well, you know, what are you talking about?"

I said, "Well, maybe we could send a ship up here, a tanker or something, and we'd pick up some fuel."

He said, "Well, maybe we can talk about that. What kind of tanker did you have in mind?"

I was really pulling it out, and I said, "Hey, we've got some MSC tankers that come into Bahrain, and, you know, perhaps we could do that."

He said, "Well, how much fuel would that be?"

I said, "Well, I think that those tankers displace around 40,000 tons, but I don't know their precise fuel load capacity."

He said, "Well, you know, we'll work out something here."

Well, at noontime, I had lunch with the Oil Minister, Sheikh Ali, who was really Fatah's boss. I brought it up to Sheikh Ali, who is no longer the Oil Minister, at lunch. By that time I had made a phone call to refine my numbers a bit, so I had a little better idea of what the hell I was talking about. It turned out that when you did some fairly liberal calculations of how much fuel all the ships engaged in the escort operation used, plus all of the fuel used by the battle group in the Indian Ocean, the carrier and its escorts, during a 30-day period, that came out very close to the amount of fuel that can be carried in one MSC ship.

Paul Stillwell: Were you interested in aviation fuel?

Admiral Bernsen: That's right, both surface ship fuel and JP-5 as well.[*] And, interestingly enough, Kuwait was the only place in the Gulf, before the Iraqi invasion, where they produced JP-5. So while we were sitting at lunch, I mentioned the MSC ship, and I mentioned the fuel capacity/requirement relationship. I said, "You know, if we could get an MSC tanker here in Kuwait, and fill it up once a month, that would in fact satisfy the requirement for the whole force. I mean, I was very careful to say, ". . . including the carrier and escorts, which are really here only in support of this escort operation," which was perhaps gilding the lily just a little but, but nevertheless pretty close to the truth.

Well, Sheikh Ali is a very interesting guy, a very decisive and very forceful guy. He didn't blink. He did not blink, other than to say, "That is a lot of fuel." And he listened, and we discussed a little further; I don't remember all the discussion. After 15-20 minutes, not very long, he got up and left the room. He came back about 15 minutes later and said we had a deal and added, "But I've got some conditions." He sat down at the table. Well, there was no doubt in my mind he either talked to one of two people or both, and that was the Prime Minister and the Emir, because I don't think that anyone in Kuwait could have offered a deal that fast without that kind of support, because we're really talking about, at then prices for JP-5, and I think we ended up about a 60-40 split for the most part, 60% surface ship, 40% aviation fuel.

Paul Stillwell: DFM for the surface ships?

---

[*] JP-5 is a type of fuel for jet aircraft. It was developed in 1952 and is notable for its high flash point, designed to minimize the risk of fire on board aircraft carriers.

Admiral Bernsen: Yes, DFM, and the other 40% was JP-5.* But it would vary. We were talking in the neighborhood of between $6 and $8 million per shipload. You're talking about some bucks here. Now, the conditions were very simple ones. He said, "There can be no paperwork. There will be no paperwork. You will bring the ship in here, tie her up, we will fill up the ship, and your liaison officer will tell us what proportion, and that ship will sail away, and there will be no paperwork. How you put that into your system will be up to you."

I'll be honest with you, I was floored, because I didn't think any of this was going to go at all. I thought it was just a stab in the dark. We shook hands, and he said, "When can you have your ship up here?"

I said, "Hopefully, in a month or less." This was in June. I went back to the flagship absolutely ecstatic. I was just on top of the world. And I had done a little mental calculation. I didn't know how long this drill was going to go on, but if we had a ship up there the next week, that until the end of the year anyway, I figured on six trips. We were talking about some $50 million worth of fuel, and I thought this was just terrific.

Well, I wrote a message and explained as simply as I could, but in some detail so hopefully, it was credible, summarizing my conversation and the deal. As a bottom line, I recommended that we get one of the four MSC ships that used to come to Bahrain periodically, and that we add it as part of one of the normal escort operations. Just tack it on the end, send it up to Kuwait, fill it up, and there we go. Then whatever you want to do with it after that is the Navy's business. I sent the message, and I was a little forward. I sent the message to Crist with info to CNO and the Chairman. That was perhaps a little impetuous, but I thought it was so important, and I felt that they needed to know this.

Crist said, "It's a logistics matter; it's an internal Navy matter. Hal, you and the CNO work this out. As far as I'm concerned, it's not a problem. It's okay." An unconscionably long time went on before MSC came up with a ship. When they did, we found out that the ship that they picked had dirty tanks. The tanks had to be cleaned on the other side of the world, and I mean it was a drill. July, August, September, three

---

* DFM – Diesel fuel marine, a light distillate fuel, as opposed to the tar-like Navy special fuel oil (NFSO) that Navy surface ships burned for many years.

months went by. No ship. I wrote a couple of messages, made some phone calls, couldn't seem to get anything off dead center, and then October showed up, and here came Admiral Brooks.

I remember one of the first things I discussed with him was the MSC ship to Kuwait to get fuel, and the answer I got was, "That's not a good idea, because it might get blown up or something. It's not a good idea." Frankly, I had so many other things on my mind that although I was very enthused about it initially, it was not one of my priorities.

Every time I went to Kuwait, Sheikh Ali would say, "Where's the ship?"

Basically I was told there wasn't going to be any. I mean, Brooks said, "Over my dead body. I'm not going to risk an MSC ship to Kuwait to get fuel."

Well, that fall, I think it was—whenever it was, October something—Admiral Trost came to visit, and one of the questions that came up was free fuel. He took me aside confidentially and said, "Why aren't you getting free fuel?"

I said, "Admiral, I've been directed not to send an MSC ship to Kuwait." Within a week, that order had been rescinded, and I began to see the paperwork for it. The CNO went back to Washington, got the whole thing unscrewed. The next thing I knew, an MSC ship came steaming up the Gulf in a convoy, and she went to Kuwait. I don't know whether it was a sixth sense or whatever, I went to Kuwait the day after she arrived, and I was sitting with the KOTC president, manager.

Somebody who worked for him came into the office very agitated, started talking in Arabic, and handed a sheaf of papers to Al Fatah. He got very irritated at me and agitated and said, "The deal's off. No fuel. That's it. You didn't follow the rules."

I said, "What the hell are you talking about?"

He said, "There are six people here from the Defense Fuels Agency with all the usual test requirements and the paperwork and all the rest of it. And you know what the rules were, very clearly, that there wasn't going to be any paperwork."

I said, "Oh, my God, I don't believe it." I had talked to the general in charge of the Defense Fuels Agency during the summertime and explained to him in detail how this thing was supposed to work, or not work in his case.

Paul Stillwell: "This is too good a deal to screw up."

Admiral Bernsen: So I didn't know what the hell to do.

I called the embassy. I got whoever their contact was at the embassy. I talked to the ambassador and explained what the problem was. I said, "You've got to turn these guys off or something." And they did. We got the paperwork torn up, and it turned out that basically what they were there for was to quality control the fuel. When the Kuwaitis said no paperwork, the DFA assumed they were talking about invoices and all that stuff. The fuels people didn't think that meant no absolutely paperwork, which is what it meant. No paperwork of any kind is what Sheikh Ali meant. These guys assumed no invoices and no charges, but they were going to do all the testing to determine quality of the fuel and have the test results all signed on the bottom line, and all the filtering and all the rest of it, whatever they do. And, of course, the deal was no paperwork, nothing, we'll just give it to you. You want to test it, you test it out there someplace. So when we finally got that sorted out, that was it. That was the first load, and it went on every month until the invasion of Kuwait. We were still getting fuel up until August 1990.

Paul Stillwell: Even though that mission had gone away.

Admiral Bernsen: Even though the mission had gone away, we were still getting a ship a month. As far as I know, if Saddam Hussein hadn't invaded Kuwait, we'd probably still be getting free fuel.* And it was so funny, because when I eventually got back to CinCLantFlt in my next tour of duty, in our fuel allocation, in our budgeting process in the comptroller's shop, they automatically every month entered a factor that was the CinCLantFlt portion of the fuel that that ship carried out of Kuwait every month. I don't think there was anybody in the budget shop that had the foggiest idea of what it was or where it came from, but only that they got this factor every month that they had to add in that was worth X number of dollars, so many gallons or barrels of fuel, whatever it was.

---

* Saddam Hussein, authoritarian President of Iraq, took power in 1979. He led his nation into a war against Iran in the 1980s, and his forces invaded Kuwait in the summer of 1990. He was toppled from power after U.S. forces invaded Iraq in 2003. He was executed in 2006.

When the invasion took place, one of the first things that happened was that the budgeteers came running down the ladder to see me and said, "The free fuel went away. What are we going to do? We can't run the fleet."

I said, "Well, I think that's the way it's going to be."

But that was a kick and, despite a lot of foot-dragging and fiddling around, it eventually worked, and I think it was greatly to our benefit. We got a lot of money out of that.

Paul Stillwell: Did Admiral Brooks back off when this order came from above?

Admiral Bernsen: Oh, yes. You see, I don't think there was ever anything in writing to me so that nothing in writing came later. The message to initiate the fuel pickup came directly from the CNO.

Paul Stillwell: Well, that in a sense absolved Admiral Brooks of responsibility, so it wasn't his worry anymore.

Admiral Bernsen: That's right. And that was the end of it. That's right. It wasn't his worry anymore, and then he got out of it. And, of course, nothing happened to the ship. It was part of the convoy; nothing was going to happen to it any more that was going to happen to anybody in any other ship. Of course, if there had been mines, I mean it would have been susceptible just like any other but no more than any other. I just felt from the beginning that it was a small risk worth taking. I mean, it was so amusing to watch the Kuwaiti reaction during the summer when they would ask us, because their feeling was they had responded so quickly to their request, why were we not taking advantage of the offer. It was made very clear to me that something must be wrong. They said, "We have offered you this fairly significant amount of free fuel, and you won't send a ship up here to get it, which means the escort operation you're running doesn't have much credibility." And I was really becoming a little paranoid because I felt my credibility was also on the line.

Paul Stillwell: Well, it was embarrassing too.

Admiral Bernsen: It was very embarrassing. That's exactly what it was. It was very embarrassing. It was as if this operation we were running was so full of holes that we didn't even want to send our own ship up there.

Paul Stillwell: Why couldn't you get the ship? Or why wouldn't MSC provide it? Do you know?

Admiral Bernsen: Oh, I think initially it was just some bureaucratic inertia; it wasn't this simple. I mean, it appeared simple initially, but in the final analysis this needed more than just the Navy to actually go forward. It needed DoD, it needed State, it needed MSC. I mean, there were a lot of people that got involved in this. I think there was a debate for a month or so, literally, at the State Department, concerning whether or not this was to our benefit. I mean, the money was to our benefit obviously, but whether diplomatically this was a good thing to do. I think there was also the age-old debate of the mercenary, much like the debate that went on during Desert Shield/Desert Storm, where all of these other people are paying us to do their job. And in '87 this was a very new concept for us. I think there were also some people in the Navy, not the CNO specifically, but probably some other people who were literally too proud to take that money. I don't know that to be a fact, but I suspect it.

Paul Stillwell: But from what you say about your conversation with Admiral Trost, it doesn't sound like he was an obstacle.

Admiral Bernsen: I don't think so, no. But I don't think that he focused on it very much during the summer, even though he was the personal addressee on that message I sent. I still have that message. It was personal for Crist, Trost, and Crowe—just those three guys. So I know he read it, but I think it sort of went out of his mind.

Paul Stillwell: He expected it to happen.

Admiral Bernsen: He gave it to one of his staff to deal with it. Well, by the time it went through DoD and the NSC, and got into State Department channels, I think it all got sort of bogged down.* I think there were an awful lot of bureaucrats who didn't understand that we were talking about a whole bunch of money every month. And every month you screwed around with this thing and you didn't do it was another month it didn't get delivered. You weren't going to get it again.

Paul Stillwell: It was lost.

Admiral Bernsen: It was gone, yes. You were not going to get two next month; it was gone. It disappeared. "You had your chance, and you didn't take it." I said $6-8 million. Actually, I think at the prices that we were looking at, at the mix we were looking at, it was more than that. I think it was $9 to $12 million. I think it was more than that, so we're talking about big sums.

Paul Stillwell: That was not crude oil; that was refined product.

Admiral Bernsen: Yes, that's right. But it eventually came off, and I saw Sheikh Ali not very long before I left in early '88. I expressed my thanks for his generous offer, and it all worked very well. And they were quite happy to do it. It represented really a pittance in their view. It wasn't very much, and they were getting a good deal. And we were being mercenary to some extent; let's face it.

Paul Stillwell: Sure a lot cheaper than all that oil that went up in smoke during the war.

Admiral Bernsen: Absolutely. If you looked at how much that 40,000-ton MSC tanker carried once a month, even though it was mostly refined product, if you looked at the number of ships in the 100,000 to 200,000-ton range that we were escorting every month, it was a drop in the bucket. I don't know what it was, 1%, 2%, something like that of what they were able to export. It wasn't a problem for them.

---

* NSC – National Security Council.

Paul Stillwell: And they didn't have to invest in a Navy or all the other things.

Admiral Bernsen: And without the paperwork and all the rest of it, it was totally deniable if the Iranians had come to them. I mean, I'm not sure why they would, or why they would even deny it, but it was, "We don't even know what you're talking about." And we could say the same thing basically too. I am amazed. I never saw it in the newspaper, not once, never. And it wasn't secret. I mean, I heard people talk about it a couple of times, but I never saw it. No reporter ever picked up on it. The Pat Tylers of the world did not glom onto this, and I really felt that if they had, they would have raised the mercenary issue.* Whether it would have embarrassed the United States Government or not, I don't know, but it certainly would have been worth an editorial in *The Post*; I'm sure of that.

Paul Stillwell: What would have been your answer if Pat Tyler asked you about it?

Admiral Bernsen: I think I would have answered him to the effect that, "Yes, the Kuwaitis do provide us fuel." But I would not have elaborated. I did see in the paper the business about the fuel barge coming out to provide fuel to the destroyer that who arrived at the northern escort station. That was in addition to the fuel picked up by the MSC tanker. That started at the very beginning and continued, because our escorts were normally below 50% fuel capacity when they reached Kuwaiti waters, and they needed to be pumped up. It had nothing to do with the tanker deal. So whenever the issue of fuel came up, that was always the way I answered, "Yes, but Kuwaitis provide us fuel. You know about those barges up there that bring fuel to our escorts." So I never lied, but I didn't give them the whole story.

Paul Stillwell: Didn't volunteer.

Admiral Bernsen: I didn't volunteer a lot of information.

---

* Patrick E. Tyler was a correspondent for *The Washington Post* from 1979 to 1990.

Interview Number 2 with Rear Admiral Harold J. Bernsen, U.S. Navy (Retired)
Place: Admiral Bernsen's office, Norfolk, Virginia
Date: Friday, 12 September 1997

Paul Stillwell: Admiral, we've had somewhat of a delay since our last interview on this. I'm delighted we're able to get back together again. Before we started here, you gave me a little background that your time in the Middle East has come up in context of a legal suit that the Iranian Government has brought, and you've had occasion to refresh your memory. I wonder if we could go back to something that we didn't really cover last time when you dealt mostly with the U.S. vis-à-vis Iran. What was the situation concerning the United States and Iraq, the attack on the *Stark*, the de-confliction procedures, and so forth.*

Admiral Bernsen: Sure. That particular incident, the *Stark* incident, because it didn't deal with Iran specifically, is not something that has come up recently with regard to what you just mentioned concerning the Iranian lawsuit against the United States that's being taken up with the World Court. As a result, it's not something that is particularly fresh in my mind. However, having said that, it was such a traumatic experience that I don't know that I can ever forget it. Most of the details, or at least a lot of them, are indelibly imprinted on my mind.

As you may recall, the incident with the *Stark* occurred on the 17th of May 1987. The 17th of May is an interesting date, because it happens to be the same date as Norwegian Independence Day, and I'm of Norwegian descent. The 17th of May is a great holiday in my house, so I always remember that. It happened to be a day when I was entertaining on board the flagship.† The flagship was tied up at the pier in Manama in Bahrain. I was wont to invite to dinner various dignitaries from the local diplomatic community, as well as some of my shipmates. That particular evening I happened to

---

* On 17 May 1987, while she was operating in the Persian Gulf, the guided missile frigate *Stark* (FFG-31) was hit by two Exocet air-to-surface missiles fired by an Iraqi Mirage F1 fighter. One of the two missiles exploded, resulting in heavy damage and fires. Of the *Stark*'s crew, 37 men were killed and 21 injured. For details, see Jeffrey L. Levinson and Randy L. Edwards, *Missile Inbound* (Annapolis: Naval Institute Press, 1997).
† USS *La Salle* (AGF-3) was flagship of Commander Middle East Force 1972 to 1980 and 1983 to 1994.

have our ambassador to Bahrain as one of my guests, Sam Zakhem.* We were sitting at dinner when the watch came down from the war room and informed me of a report from the Air Force AWACS that was flying out of Saudi Arabia.† The report was that an Iraqi aircraft had been detected and was coming south out of Iraq. That was not unusual. I won't say it was normal but almost normal.

Paul Stillwell: What was the context at that point? What were they doing, and what was our role?

Admiral Bernsen: Let me go back just a little bit. That dinner always focuses me a little bit, but I think it's probably useful to go back a couple of days. We would have to do that anyway in order to get the full picture. We had a station in the northern half of the Persian Gulf, northeast of Farsi Island.‡ At that station we placed a surface combatant most of the time to monitor the activity of the Iraqi aircraft that were coming down from the north and were then turning to the east. They would come down from Baghdad and the airfields around Baghdad and skirt the western edge of the northern Gulf. Then at some point, which we surmised was a point where they detected on their air-to-surface radar a shipping contact, presumably Iranian, along the Iranian coast to the east, they would then turn east and launch a missile at that contact.

There was no identification procedure that was followed. It was simply a blind shot. The fact is on many occasions they actually hit. These were Exocet missiles, and they actually were able to strike the target.§ The Exocet is an extremely good missile, and the French had supplied the Iraqis with a good many of them, and they were practiced in their use. Normally, after the aircraft carrying the missile had turned east or southeast, it would fly a sufficient distance, namely into the center of the Gulf or even further east than the center of the Gulf, so that at launch it was no more than 20 or 25 miles away from its intended target, whatever they happened to see on the radar screen. And those ships—principally Iranian tankers, which were the big targets—were pretty

---

* Dr. Sam Zakhem was U.S. ambassador to Bahrain from 1986 to 1989.
† AWACS – airborne warning and control system. This is an aerial look-down radar and tracking system carried on board the Air Force's E-3 Sentry, a modified Boeing 707 airliner with a rotating radome on top.
‡ Farsi Island serves as a base for the Iranian Navy.
§ Exocet is a French-made antiship missile that can be fired from surface ships, submarines, and airplanes.

close to the coast of Iran. Now, what had happened three days before the *Stark* incident—and I may be a day off on that, I'd say it was three to four days prior—the USS *Coontz* was up on that station. An Iraqi Exocet-carrying, we assume—an Iraqi aircraft in any case—had come down out of Iraq from Baghdad. It had been detected by the AWACS, the AWACS reported this contact to the *Coontz*, and the *Coontz* then did all of the things that they were briefed to do. They acquired the contact on radar, they tracked it into a point at which the rules of engagement said they were supposed to warn the pilot on the radio that if his aircraft proceeded any further, that he would be at a risk of being taken under fire. That warning was, in fact, given.

Paul Stillwell: In English?

Admiral Bernsen: In English. At a distance, as I recall, of something like 50 miles the Iraqi turned around and went home. The path that he was predicted to take would have taken him just over the *Coontz*. The assumption then is that he would have turned to the east and gone after some target along the coast, but he never did that. He turned around, and he went home.

Now, what's different here is that—and I have to go back and correct myself—that particular station had not been occupied on a regular basis, so being warned didn't happen to the Iraqis on a regular basis. We didn't have a ship there, so therefore they didn't get any warning, because they weren't approaching a U.S. ship in that position. Most of our ships were much further south. But in this case we had a ship there. When the ship's radar and the various folks in CIC who were responsible saw this, including the ship's captain, who was quite involved in this whole procedure, all of the steps were followed.* The aircraft was followed on radar, it was given the appropriate warnings, the fire control radar, as I recall, on *Coontz* was actually aimed at the Iraqi fighter, and I'm sure he got a couple of indications in the cockpit that he was being lit up, and at that point the pilot turned around, and he turned around well outside of Exocet range. About 50 miles, as I recall.

---

* Commander William W. Cobb Jr., USN, commanded the guided missile destroyer *Coontz* (DDG-40) from 11 April 1987 to 21 July 1989.

Paul Stillwell: What was the purpose of having a U.S. ship there?

Admiral Bernsen: We were up there simply observing the situation, ship traffic and how things were working and going on. There may have been some other more specific reason, but I don't recall, to be honest about it, and it's probably where I'm a little hazy on that one.

Paul Stillwell: Was there a rule of engagement that covered that?

Admiral Bernsen: The rules of engagement were exactly the same as they would have been any place in the Gulf. Those were our standard rules. In this case it was clearly an Iraqi aircraft, because it had been identified by the AWACS and the AWACS radar. The rule said that if you had either an Iraqi or an Iranian aircraft, and he was approaching you at certain mileage points, you had certain things that you needed to do. You could just read them off a piece of paper. This was a promulgated rule of engagement vetted by CentCom. It was my set of rules, but it had been vetted by everybody in the United States military hierarchy, I'm convinced. Maybe even the President. In fact, the President, after the *Stark* incident, as you may recall, did get into the business of rules of engagement. But the other thing that was in that rule was that in fact if that Iraqi aircraft had failed to turn around and had continued to fly directly toward that ship, the ship was empowered to destroy that aircraft. Now, in this particular case the airplane turned around, and essentially that was the end of the incident.

Paul Stillwell: In the case of the *Coontz*?

Admiral Bernsen: Yes. *Coontz*—she vacated the station the next day. *Coontz* came back to Bahrain, tied up at the pier. *Stark* came to Bahrain and tied up at the pier. On the 15th, at my morning briefing, as we normally did, we invited the skippers who were in the area to come aboard and join us. The skipper of the *Stark* was at that morning briefing.* I can't remember whether it was the staff intelligence officer or the ops officer who gave the brief; I think it was the intelligence officer. He gave a little thumbnail of what had occurred two nights before with the *Coontz*, emphasizing certain details. At the conclusion of that briefing I turned to the skipper of the *Stark*, and I said, "You know, you're going up there." *Stark* was assigned to go to that position that day. They were going to leave Bahrain later that morning. I said, "You're going to go up there. We've already talked about rules of engagement, but why don't you sit down with my people right after the brief and get the full story of everything that went on up there." And in fact that's what he did.

Paul Stillwell: That was Captain Brindel.

Admiral Bernsen: Yes. My staff people had the full story and all of the transcripts and all the rest of it, but Brindel was instructed to sit down and go over the report of the incident in greater detail with my people. Clearly I made the point. It wasn't something that was an "Oh, by the way." It was clearly, "This is what you need to do, because you might have a situation like this occur again." Later that morning Brindel, in the *Stark*, departed Bahrain and moved north. They were in that position that evening of the 17th where I began the story, but that's the context.

What the duty officer came down and told me was that an aircraft had been picked up by the AWACS and that it was headed south, and my only question to the watch officer was, "Is *Stark* aware, and are they in communication with AWACS?"

The answer was, "Yes, they are." At that point I felt reasonably comfortable with the situation, if it played out in accordance with the way it should have played out. Brindel, I was reasonably certain, had specifically been briefed on what happened just a few nights before. He knew the rules of engagement. At the outset the situation appeared to be similar to what developed with *Coontz*. But when I was first informed, the aircraft was still 100 miles away or more from the *Stark*. If the aircraft didn't turn around, then I was sure that the duty officer would come down and tell me real quick. But there wasn't really a great deal that I or my staff could do, other than to make sure

---

* Captain Glenn R. Brindel, USN, was commanding officer of the *Stark*.

that the *Stark* was aware of the situation, and I was assured that they were, and in fact they were.

Paul Stillwell: Did somebody on your staff communicate specifically with the *Stark*?

Admiral Bernsen: Yes. Yes. That's what the duty officer came down to tell me, "We have queried the *Stark*; we have asked the *Stark* if they are listening to the AWACS transmissions, and if they are aware of the Iraqi aircraft that's coming south, and the answers to all of those questions were positive." Then there was one more quick visit by the duty officer. Unfortunately, the next duty officer visit was to inform me that something horrible had happened, that something had gone drastically wrong. At that point I leaped up from the table and ran up to the war room, where the command duty officer was. The ambassador was right behind me.

We stood up there and listened to reports on the radio from the *Stark*, and she had obviously been hit, devastated. From then on it's a blur. I can't even begin to tell you all the different things that occurred, but we rushed ships from where we could find them. One or two ships in Bahrain got under way, I don't remember their names, and moved north toward the *Stark*. The ambassador immediately alerted the Bahraini Government, and in fact the Bahraini launched helicopters at night, which was not their normal procedure, to look for people in the water. We, of course, had our own helicopters out there, and we began to get the flagship under way. The dinner party obviously was finished. The guests were moved ashore very quickly, and the ship made preparations to get under way.

Paul Stillwell: Did you initiate any communication with the Iraqi Government?

Admiral Bernsen: No. I had no means of directly communicating with the Iraqi Government. That was not something that I had. What I had done in the past, prior to that time, was I had communicated with our military mission in Baghdad by phone, but I think we talked like twice. It was not a routine circumstance, and I certainly didn't have any way to contact them by radio. And I had no way to contact the Iraqi Government or any military unit in the Iraqi military directly. As I said, our embassy possibly could. At that point I wasn't concerned. I was so taken up with what the hell had happened with the *Stark*. We got under way, went to sea. Other ships beat us to it, of course, which we expected. But we steamed out, and we were not very far away from the *Stark*. By the time we arrived, the fires had been put out. There were still people unaccounted for, people in the water. It was just devastation. There was smoke but none of the actual flames.

Paul Stillwell: I thought some of the *La Salle* people contributed to the damage control effort.

Admiral Bernsen: Oh, yes. Although by the time we got there, of course, one of the things that became immediately apparent was that the ship's company people who had been fighting this conflagration all night long—and we're talking about the ship being hit something like 8:30, 9:00 o'clock the night before. I can't remember the exact minute but something like that. Obviously all night—they were getting very tired. They were exhausted, so what all the ships did, and certainly *La Salle*, having one of the largest complements out there, was that we contributed people to the effort. They actually sent damage control teams over to the *Stark* to relieve the people that were on board who were totally exhausted, brought them back over to *La Salle*, gave them showers and gave them some food and put them to bed and that sort of thing, if they could sleep.

I have only positive things to say about the performance of the people on board *Stark* as far as damage control is concerned. I think that the investigation later on showed without any equivocation that they did a masterful job. There were some, I think, very noteworthy instances of bravery, of people who entered very potentially dangerous areas to rescue other sailors, to take care of the whole situation and to rescue the ship because, of course, the ship didn't go down. It survived. I think that is a direct result of a well-drilled ship and some very dedicated folks. I don't think there's any doubt about that. I would not fault Captain Brindel or his executive officer or anyone else on the ship as to that aspect of their performance.

The issue that disturbed me and came to disturb me more and more as the investigation progressed—and the investigation, let me be clear, began rather quickly after the incident. When 37 people die, the Navy gets pretty disturbed; everybody gets disturbed. The Persian Gulf, at that point in time, was not a very popular place, as you recall. There was a considerable amount of discussion in the Congress about our presence in the Gulf, whether it was warranted and to what degree, how many ships and so forth. The administration, on the other hand, had taken the position that our presence in the Gulf was necessary.

Paul Stillwell: Well, you laid some of that groundwork in our last interview, talking about the debates on whether we should have it, and finally it was the Kuwaitis going to the Soviets that kind of triggered us into it.

Admiral Bernsen: That's right. But despite all that, there was still a very significant body of opinion in the Congress, as well as probably a few in the administration, who said, "This is a bad place to be. It is too dangerous for us, and we're going to get caught in the crossfire." Well, boy, here we had it. *Stark* gets hit with a missile, and the Iraqis shoot the missile, and the Iraqis were less our enemy than the Iranians. In fact, we weren't exactly upfront friendly with them, but certainly we sympathized with the Iraqis. Whenever the Iranians were winning, our sympathies with the Iraqis seemed to grow, at least back in Washington.

It was just an extraordinary situation, and what the hell are you going to do about it? The plane is gone. The Iraqis at first didn't even acknowledge that it happened and over a period of time never volunteered the pilot, of course, but maintained that it was a total error, it was a mistake, and he certainly hadn't intended to do that. And a case can be made for that explanation.

But back to the investigation. Within a very few days, an investigating officer had been designated, Grant Sharp, and a team had been put together and were flown out to Bahrain.[*] I was informed that they would take up residence on the flagship, and I was directed to make appropriate space available, which I did. Grant Sharp, who interestingly

---

[*] Rear Admiral Grant A. Sharp, USN, Commander Cruiser-Destroyer Group Two.

enough, I did not know very well—I think I'd met him once before—was a very distinguished and competent surface officer. I've gotten to know him much, much better in succeeding years. We've worked together since retirement, as a matter of fact, a number of times. But Grant had a reputation as a no-nonsense guy, and I think during the association I had with him on the flagship that was brought home in spades. He was a no-nonsense guy. But certainly there was no antagonism there. What he brought with him was a very professional desire to get on with this investigation and find out what really happened.

Paul Stillwell: Businesslike approach.

Admiral Bernsen: Very businesslike approach. Came to see me in my cabin immediately and then quite on purpose, I'm sure, elected to have his own mess. We did not see each other except for very few times after that.

Paul Stillwell: What would you say was his motive in that?

Admiral Bernsen: At the particular time when he came aboard, I think Grant recognized full well that there could have been a whole host of causes for this incident, not the least of which might have been the non-performance or questionable performance of the commander, namely me. I don't think that he wanted to put himself or me in a position where anyone could ever say that I had wrongly influenced him or the board.

Paul Stillwell: I see.

Admiral Bernsen: Now, his people interviewed every one of my officers, and he interviewed me. The investigation, as I recall, went on for some ten days, maybe even a bit longer than that. Just before he left the ship he came in, and he said, "We're finished. We're going to go home, and we're going to write this thing up."

I had the temerity to say, "Grant, I don't know if you're allowed to do this, but how did we come out here on the staff, because I am concerned?"

He said, "Not a problem. I had no problem with your actions or the actions of your staff. The preparation and the briefings that were provided to the skipper of the *Stark* were appropriate and in my view sufficient for him to have taken the proper action." Now, that corresponded, surprisingly, with my own view, but it was very nice to hear that from the senior investigating officer.

Paul Stillwell: Reassuring.

Admiral Bernsen: Reassuring and, yes, we are all careerists to some degree at least, and I was hoping I wasn't going to get fired the next day. So when I did see the actual investigation I was pleased to note that neither me personally or the staff had come under any particular criticism at all. Now, what really did happen—this is what's the disturbing part—it seems that when Captain Brindel got back to his ship after the morning brief on the flagship, that he did not gather his CIC team, his operations officer, or any of the other key people together and go over with them the events that had occurred previously on board *Coontz*. Why he did not do that I don't know. Now, in the interviews that he underwent during the investigation, he maintained over and over again that he was so focused on the need to conduct a series of engineering drills for his superiors back in the United States that the rest of the mission, quite frankly, came second.

Now, I understand Captain Brindel's concern about getting those drills done and done properly, because the ship was going to go back and enter an OPPE phase.[*] A lot of these tests had something to do with that and were certainly not part of the operational commander's scheme. I recognized that ships had to do these things, obviously. So did aircraft squadrons. But, on the other hand, when put in harm's way, clearly that station up there was a difficult one and one that was subject to threat. I honestly believe in retrospect that Captain Brindel was putting the cart before the horse—that he had the wrong thing on his mind. Anyway, for whatever the reason, he didn't brief his people. As a result, although they should have known and did know as they testified, the rules of engagement, they were not aware of the fact that Iraqi aircraft had appeared to threaten

---

[*] OPPE – operational propulsion plant examination, a demanding inspection of training, procedures, equipment, and personnel.

the *Coontz* a couple of days before. They weren't aware of the sequence of events, and they weren't aware of the fact that after the rules of engagement had been applied correctly and in accordance with the directives, that the Iraqi had actually turned around and gone home. Well, anyone who has read the investigation recognizes that—I guess it was that young lieutenant down there who literally didn't want to make waves.* He didn't want to get up on the radio and tell anybody anything, so they just let the airplane fly down their throats. By the time somebody recognized that they potentially had a very serious situation developing very quickly, it was too late.

Paul Stillwell: He was not apparently alerted by the message from your staff to be aware of this.

Admiral Bernsen: And the skipper was in the head, on the potty, during most of this evolution. The others, the exec, the ops officer, etc., who could have taken some sort of action either didn't concern themselves with the problem. Or they were otherwise involved with these engineering trials and drills, or flat didn't pay any attention. I really fault the skipper. I think there are other people who certainly could have done something to prevent this, but it really emanated in this case from the top on down. A terrible tragedy, but it just shows what a lack of priorities and command attention can do for you. Something as obvious as passing the word. I mean, I as the flag would not have told him to stay on after that briefing for an extra 20 minutes to get the details if I had not felt that it was critical. We wouldn't have emphasized the importance of the incident. Instead, we would have made note of it and said, "Yeah, that's fine, and let's go on to the next thing," but it was critical. It was clear to everyone involved in my circle that we had a different situation here—perhaps not a major obvious difference but somewhat of a difference in tactic here. We were putting a ship in a position which we had not put a ship in before except for *Coontz* the first time, and that the ship might very well end up encountering an Iraqi airplane.

---

* Lieutenant Basil E. Moncrief, USN, was the *Stark*'s tactical action officer.

Paul Stillwell: I think you told me once before that Bill Cobb had done well. Was he the CO of *Coontz*?

Admiral Bernsen: You got it. That's precisely the point, and I've talked to Bill about it a number of times in the years since. And Bill says, "You know, there but for the Grace of God go I."

I said, "No, that's not true, Bill. It wasn't going to happen to you, because you used common sense." I mean, procedures are procedures but common sense comes into play as well. When you know that that is the way in which the Iraqis have been running their air attack operation, when you know that they only get a radar target and fire on the target, not on identification, and you're in the area within 30 to 40 miles, which is not a very great distance, certainly from an airplane point of view, 30 to 40 miles from where ships are being attacked, certainly you could come under attack unless you are very forceful in explaining to that guy in the air that, "Listen, Buddy, you come down here any closer, and I'm going to shoot you out of the air." And that was what Cobb did. He did the whole thing—the fire control radar, the oral warnings—and the Iraqi turned around.

Paul Stillwell: Well, the being illuminated by the fire control radar should do it even if the oral warning is not understood.

Admiral Bernsen: The *Stark* didn't do any of that. Never gave any oral warnings. Yes, they acquired the guy on the fire control radar but only after the pilot was close in and had fired his missiles. Simply did not comply with the rules of engagement. After all was said and done and all the excuses and all of the this and all of the that, that's basically what Grant Sharp came down to. In this obviously critical situation, potentially high-threat environment, potentially very dangerous situation, that the procedures which were laid down to precisely apply in that kind of a situation were simply ignored from the top down. No one likes to make that kind of a judgment, but later on when Brindel, I think, and his XO were seeking mitigation to counter the punitive administrative action that had been taken by the Navy, namely that he had been essentially fired, thrown out of the Navy, he was looking for reinstatement or getting his grade back, maybe that was it.[*] I thought to myself, "He got off very lightly."

Paul Stillwell: I think he was temporarily a captain.

Admiral Bernsen: Yes, and he retired as a commander. But, I mean, clearly the man had in fact not lived up to the responsibility he was given. Clearly. A very sad situation and probably the saddest, or at least the most moving, day of my life was on the tarmac at Bahrain International Airport when each of those 36 flag-draped coffins moved up the ramp on that C-141 for the flight home.[†] And, of course, what goes through your mind at that point, regardless of what the hell any investigation says or whether you officially have been exonerated, all you do is you stand there and you say, "Was there anything else that we could have done that might have avoided this goddamn thing?"

Paul Stillwell: You got a sick feeling in your gut.

Admiral Bernsen: It's a terrible feeling. And it's a sick feeling today. It will always be a sick feeling, and there's never been anything like it in my life. I know there were a few other incidents out there where we had loss of life, and there were incidents where we caused loss of life on the part of the Iranians, but certainly we had nothing to compare with the *Stark*. The night after, when the flagship was still out with *Stark*, I was asked to return to Bahrain and used our helo to bring me back. I think we were 30-40 miles off the coast at that point. We had the news conference that took place in one of the hotels in Bahrain, and I think there were some 40 journalists. Have you read *Primary Colors*?[‡]

---

[*] In July 1987 the Navy announced that it would not court-martial any of the *Stark*'s officers. Instead, Brindel agreed to retire at the reduced rank of commander, and Moncrief agreed to resign his officer's commission. Both received letters or reprimand.
[†] The C-141 Starlifter, a jet cargo aircraft, transported the bodies of 36 crew members to Rhein-Main Air Force Base in Germany and later to the military mortuary at Dover, Delaware. The body of one crewman was lost at sea.
[‡] *Primary Colors* is a political novel published in January 1996 and initially attributed to an anonymous author. The author was later revealed to be Joe Klein, a reporter who covered politics. The main character, Jack Stanton, is a thinly disguised version of Bill Clinton, who was President at the time of publication.

Paul Stillwell: Yes.

Admiral Bernsen: The scorpions were there. The scorps were there, and they were looking for blood. Mine. No question about it. I mean, 37 U.S. servicemen had been killed, some son of a bitch was responsible, and I was it. That—outside of the carrying away of the caskets—was the most emotional and disturbing part to me, but probably the second most traumatic experience of my life was facing that group of journalists that evening.

Paul Stillwell: How well acquainted were they collectively on Navy procedures and such things?

Admiral Bernsen: They didn't know anything, because you remember clearly that we hadn't begun Earnest Will at this point, so—relatively speaking—there had been very little press concentration and coverage on the Gulf. Nothing like began after the *Stark* or was initiated at *Stark* and continued on during the whole escort mission when, of course, we had reporters on every ship and all the rest of it. At that point in time we had this huge gaggle of people that were flown to the area from all over the place. Stringers from Europe and the Far East who were told by their news organizations, "Get your butt to Bahrain and cover this thing." I would say that we probably had two or three people in the whole world that had any clue as to what the Navy was all about or what airplanes were all about or missiles or anything else, so you can imagine what the questions were.

Admiral Bernsen: All over the ballpark.

Admiral Bernsen: They were all over the ballpark. The tone was not friendly, and the bottom line was, "Somebody's responsible, and we've got the guy right here in front of us, and, by God, he's going to 'fess up."

Paul Stillwell: What was the tone or nature of your response?

Admiral Bernsen: Somebody told me that I did reasonably well. I don't know. It was under very bright lights, because it had been set up by the Minister of Information of Bahrain, who by the way was not happy about any of this. He didn't want anybody to say that this news conference was taking place in Bahrain, because he wanted Bahrain to be kept totally out of the picture here.

Paul Stillwell: Well, they were in an uncomfortable position.

Admiral Bernsen: They were. Oh, it was a very understandable wish, and I was very aware of it. It so happened that the Minister of Information was one of my best friends in Bahrain. Still is, although he's not the Minister of Information anymore. Although at that time we were friends socially, we had a couple of run-ins professionally, because he was very concerned about this sort of thing. But he did give us permission, and once he had given his permission then the people in the embassy were able to set up the room, and the public affairs officer who was in charge was able to orchestrate this thing in some fashion. Orchestration I'm not sure is the proper word. It was a mad affair.

I said that the journalists were looking for me. I must say that's not totally true. Yes, certainly they were interested in what I might have had to do with this thing and the fact that, overall, I was responsible. But the other thing that they were trying to get at very clearly was that Iraq and an Iraqi pilot had done this on purpose. That this was a conscious act and that here we had another phase, if you will, of this war at sea, and no longer was it just Iran-Iraq. It very much concerned us, and wasn't this a plot? Wasn't this a purposeful act on the part of the Iraqis? And that's the one thing I remember out of the entire conference, was to reiterate—and I'm sure that I said it many times in various ways—that we had no indication, no proof at that time, this was a conscious act on the part of the Iraqi pilot. That didn't rule out the possibility that it could have been, but that at that particular time and place we did not know that, and it would depend on our full investigation.

What I also tried to concentrate on, which was very difficult, because the questioners weren't allowing me to do that, was the performance of the crew after the missile had struck. The performance of all of the other ships and the crews that came to help. The performance of the helicopter pilots and the Bahraini Government who had gone out and literally had rescued people out of the water. I think a commander under those circumstances, before he has any of the facts, has to try and look at the incident, not sweep it away but simply pick out those kinds of things that he is aware of personally, that are incontrovertible, and that he can speak about in some kind of a positive manner. If you will recall, it was about a year after that when the *Vincennes* shot down an airliner.* You will never forget nor will I, I'm sure, the interview of Admiral Crowe the next morning on national TV.

Paul Stillwell: Shooting from the hip.

Admiral Bernsen: Well, you know, he thought he was providing good info. He obviously in retrospect was providing a lot of nonsense. I happen to know Bill Crowe very well. Very well. I just saw him a couple of months ago in London.† I think if you read his book, too, I mean it was devastating, because he just didn't have the answers.‡ When you don't have the answers you really are hanging it out there if you just conjecture. I was trying my best not to do that. As a result, although it may not have been the best interview in the world at that point, I could have cared less whether it was good or wasn't good or considered good or not good. What I really wanted to do was to not say anything that would either impugn anyone falsely or come back to haunt our government. I didn't want to make statements that simply weren't fact. I never got any feedback. I never got any criticism from within the chain of command about that interview, which was carried all over the place, and I never got any negative feedback from others outside the chain, so I felt that that probably wasn't so bad. I'd come off pretty doggone well.

Paul Stillwell: No news is good news.

---

* On 3 July 1988, Iran Air flight 655, an A300 airbus en route from Bandar Abbas Airport to Dubai, United Arab Emirates, was destroyed by two SM-2 Standard missiles launched at a range of nine miles by the Aegis cruiser *Vincennes* (CG-49). All 290 persons on board the civilian airliner died.
† After he retired from the Navy, Crowe served from 1994 to 1997 as Ambassador to the United Kingdom.
‡ For details, see William J. Crowe Jr., *The Line of Fire: From Washington to the Gulf, the Politics and Battles of the New Military* (New York: Simon & Schuster, 1993).

Admiral Bernsen: That's right. That's not always how it worked, however. Now, certainly after the *Stark* we were inundated with the press, and immediately we got right into the middle of the age-old question: how much access should the press be allowed? How much vetting should occur? That is, should we read the copy, should we censor it? What do we do? Do we take them out on our ships? Whom do we take out? Do we take anybody that wants to come who says he's a member of the press corps? Again, as you probably are well aware, this led to one of the first really in-depth evaluations within DoD since Vietnam of just how the heck we deal with these people, and at first it was chaos. There's no question about it. It was chaos. And for a whole host of reasons. Some of them are the ones I've just given you but also the fact that the majority of the people that came out didn't have a clue as to what we were doing. As a result, they generally came out with a pretty negative point of view, and you can't expect that in one or two days you're going to change it. Many of the journalists that came out initially stayed for a long time. They might have gone home for a period of vacation but came back and came back and came back.

By the time they had been back once or twice or by the time they had steamed up the Gulf on an escort mission for a week, it was amazing to me how the attitude changed. Initially they were very negative, very suspicious, and distrustful of the quote military mind and all the rest. They believed they were going to be fed nonsense and obfuscation and all the rest. Instead, they found that what they were dealing with were really a bunch of guys trying to do a job, and they could see that the crews were doing it professionally, notwithstanding *Stark*, and they found that wherever possible we were giving them as much information as we possibly could.

Paul Stillwell: Did you put out some kind of policy of openness in dealing with the media?

Admiral Bernsen: I did, and I was basically told by some folks back in Washington that I didn't have any business to do that. They were going to make those decisions. One of the guys involved in all that was Dan Howard, who was either assistant or head of the

DoD Public Affairs Office.* I think they were more worried about all this back there than I was worried about it. Now, there was one thing that I absolutely demanded initially. I'm not sure that this was true in every case right up until the time I left, but certainly it was the first few months after the *Stark*. All of the journalists were brought to see me personally.

Paul Stillwell: Did you have an accreditation policy?

Admiral Bernsen: Oh, yes. That was all handled by the DoD folks. They sent a public affairs officer out to assist mine. Well, I didn't have one, quite frankly, so basically I got one, and over a period of time I got two or three, a commander, a lieutenant commander, a lieutenant, and a few enlisted. Well, what would happen is the journalists would be vetted in the States, put on an airplane, taken out as a group, and then they'd be taken over for their care and feeding by my own folks.

One of the very first things after they got settled was that if the flagship was available—and most of the time it was whenever we were at sea or at the pier—the group and that could be anywhere from two or three singles to maybe five or six journalists at a time, would literally be ushered in to see me, or if that was impossible I'd go see them wherever they were. I would give them about 30 minutes of how I looked at the war and what it was we were doing and as much about rules of engagement as I could in about 30 minutes, 40 minutes, about as long as anybody can expect to sit still. Now, how much of that they took aboard, probably 20%. But what it did do, I hope, and I think I was told later, was that at least it indicated to them that the boss was concerned.

I made it very clear that they were welcome. I made it very clear up front, principal point, "I want you to tell our story to the American public. We don't have anything to hide out here other than the routes of our escorts. We're not going to give you those, because that might fall in the hands of somebody else inadvertently, but just about anything else we can tell you about. The sailors are going to be as open as they possibly can be, because that's what I'm going to ask them to do. The skippers will be

---

* J. Daniel Howard served as Assistant Secretary of Defense for Public Affairs from February 1988 to May 1989. He was subsequently Under Secretary of the Navy, 1989-93,

the same, and if you find that not to be true I really would like to know about it." And I was quite serious. "Now, all of that means that we have a reciprocal relationship, and if you're going to publish something that is very critical I really would appreciate it if you would sit down and talk to me."

Paul Stillwell: Did that approach achieve the results you wanted?

Admiral Bernsen: Yes, by and large it did, with one or two exceptions. The one that I really remember had to do again with me personally. Those are the things you always remember best. This occurred with one of those journalists that ended up becoming very, very knowledgeable about the Gulf war and came out there month after month after month but on his first trip didn't know anything about what was going on.

Paul Stillwell: Is there a name you want to insert here?

Admiral Bernsen: I'm not going to insert his name. Frankly, I'm not sure if I can remember his name, although it's on the tip of my tongue, but he was a reporter at the time. He was based in Europe, as I recall.

Paul Stillwell: Was this electronic, magazine, newspaper?

Admiral Bernsen: He was a newspaper reporter, regular journalist. We were going to have a short interview on the flagship, but things got busy, and it didn't happen. The flagship was anchored outside of Bahrain, and I was going to go ashore. That was about a 30-minute trip, 35-minute trip, in my barge. He asked if he could come along, and I said, "Sure." So we both sat in the stern sheets, drove in to the beach, and he conducted his interview. We talked about escort ships. It was the very beginning of the escorts. It was probably June, and it was hot.

Paul Stillwell: That was even before the escort had started.

Admiral Bernsen: Yes, but we were talking about the concept, what we were going to do. We were in the planning stages, and that was pretty well known and so forth. The U.S. Government had agreed to do this, and this was how we were going to do it and so forth. One question out of this entire interview was about Iran-Contra.* My response very quickly, in very few words, was, "Well, you know, sending those folks over to Iran probably didn't help me carry out my mission very well."

The next day in the *Stars and Stripes* in Europe the headline was, "Admiral says Mission to Iran Jeopardizes His Mission" or whatever, something like that. That was what he picked out of that whole conversation, and that's what he wrote about. All of the rest of this business about how many ships we were bringing to the Gulf to conduct the escort mission and how our mission there, our purpose there, was to preserve stability in the Gulf region and maintain U.S. interests and all of the rest of this—that just never got in the paper at all. The only thing that got in there was, "Admiral says—" you know, that so-and-so.

Paul Stillwell: I can believe that the U.S. supplying arms to Iran did not help you.

Admiral Bernsen: It didn't. It certainly didn't. It wasn't at that particular point in time, however, an issue that I was particularly interested in either talking about or getting involved in. It was the CentCom Commander, the four-star down there, who was concerned about that. I got a couple of phone calls on that one. Anyway, as they became more familiar with what was going on, became convinced of the professionalism of the people that were involved, and I can't stress that enough, over a period of time those journalists who were out there for longer than just a few days became friendly. They truly did. And pretty soon it was like reading stuff coming out of a Navy PAO. I was amazed at some of the really positive things that were written about the mission, about the sailors, and all the rest. Now, naturally the politics of it all, whether the government really supported Iraq, the importance of keeping the oil flowing, supporting the Gulf

---

* Iran-Contra was a political scandal in the mid-1980s, during the Reagan Administration. The United States was selling arms to Iran, an avowed enemy. The proceeds from those sales were then diverted to the Contras, anti-Communist guerrillas in Nicaragua. Both the sale of the arms and the aid to the Contras violated stated administration policy and congressional legislation. From early May to early August of 1987 Congress conducted televised hearings into the affair.

Arabs, some of whom were questionable allies and not particularly likable despots—was all of what we were doing really in the national interest?

Paul Stillwell: As events later proved.

Admiral Bernsen: Yes. That kind of thing occasionally came into these articles and was questioned, and I certainly couldn't gainsay that. I mean, that was the reporter's privilege. But assuming you've decided that this is your mission and you're going to perform it, the comments concerning how we perform it and the mission itself and how it was organized were almost universally positive.

Paul Stillwell: One unintended consequence was that the favorable press coverage generated a great deal of goodwill from the American public that built the morale of those sailors.

Admiral Bernsen: There's no question about that. I think if you just toted up the number of high schools that adopted ships and sent Christmas packages and all of this other stuff that went on, it really was a very encouraging and heartwarming situation. And the sailors, no question they appreciated it. It wasn't a lot of fun out there. While most of them got into Bahrain or Dubai once or twice during a Gulf tour, there wasn't a hell of a lot of liberty. If it was during the wintertime, then it wasn't all that bad, but remember this whole business of escorting began just at the beginning of the very hottest period. *Stark* was in May. It was already hot. June it's 100, and from there on out until the end of October it's uncomfortable. Not a pleasant place to be.

Now, years ago before we had air-conditioning—in fact, when I was first there in 1980 in *La Salle*, the standard operating procedure in the Middle East force was that ships left the Gulf in the summer. They went south to places like Mombasa, which although actually closer to the equator are a heck of a lot cooler in the summertime because of the currents that flow up from Antarctica. The Gulf was not a place you wanted to hang around in during the summer months, and yet here we were in the midst of this mission, and it was right in the middle of the summer. So that complicated things.

Paul Stillwell: Did that heat cause operational difficulties with equipment?

Admiral Bernsen: Generally speaking it did not. Of far greater concern were dust and sand. You can get sandstorms throughout the year. The shamal, which is the famous north wind, normally occurs more in the winter time and early spring, March, April, when you can get 20-30-40 knots of wind right off the desert in the north, off Saudi and Iraq, and literally clouds of dust will come down. But it's gritty dust, it is sand, and it gets on all of those shiny bits on a ship, the recoil mechanisms on guns, all those kinds of places that are exposed. It gets sucked into those engine intakes, particularly in our turbine engines, which most of our ships are powered by these days and were then. As a result, over the years what has developed is a whole package of things that ships going to the Gulf do before they even arrive.

Paul Stillwell: Air filters?

Admiral Bernsen: Exactly. Air filters and special lubricants and all the rest of that but principally air filters to keep the stuff from going down to the engine room. So those things were necessary, they were being done, and I don't think anybody didn't have that protection even at that point, because we'd been sending ships to the Gulf for some time. Oh, we had five or six ships in the Gulf for a long time prior to the Earnest Will mission. Most of our ships today are air-conditioned. Now, when you're faced with a 110, 115, 120 degrees, normal air-conditioning aboard Navy ships leaves something to be desired, so I won't tell you that in the compartments it wasn't 85, and it certainly was, but it was not 110 or 115. So you could sleep, function, take showers, and for the most part people survived pretty well. They'd go out on deck for as short a period as they possibly could, and then they'd come running right back in again. I suspect there was some topsides maintenance and painting that didn't get done, but I'm not so sure that that was all that big a deal frankly. So generally I wouldn't put too much of an emphasis on that.

It's amazing. If it had been 40 years ago, we would have been concerned about a whole different set of environmental problems. Our concern was not about sand that much or heat but about radar ducting, those kinds of things. During the summer months you have a serious ducting problem in the Gulf because of these very high temperatures and the gradients so that radars do very funny things. You can in some cases pick up targets at great ranges, and in other cases you can't pick up jack. Very difficult. And so that was of very great concern to us. That was particularly of concern, as I say, during hot weather, whereas some of those other things weren't of such concern. Forty years ago it would have been totally different.

Paul Stillwell: Well, the Navy had less concern about habitability 40 years ago.

Admiral Bernsen: That's true. And let's face it. Our sailors 40 years ago didn't expect as much.

Paul Stillwell: And the equipment was cruder, too, so it wasn't as sensitive.

Admiral Bernsen: That's right. That's right. So you certainly had to worry about the dust, and you had to make sure those filters were in place and all the rest of that, but as long as you did all the kinds of recommended maintenance and installed those things, things went pretty well.

Paul Stillwell: What measures did you institute to prevent another *Stark* problem from happening?

Admiral Bernsen: As a result of the *Stark* tragedy, we took a look, as did the investigating board, at the rules of engagement and weighed them. The official determination was that if the rules of engagement had been followed, we wouldn't have had a *Stark* incident, and that was the basic response from the field back to Washington. Well, that didn't fly. A lot of people said, "Yeah, but, there has to be something else we can do." Here I became sort of an interested onlooker, because I was not consulted, I was not asked. The next thing I knew, President Ronald Reagan came up on television and said that he had changed the rules of engagement. He told the commander that the next time a situation like this occurred, the ship or unit in question had full authority to shoot down the enemy.

Fact of the matter is we already had it. We had that authority. It was in our rules of engagement, and in fact that is why our rules of engagement were constantly under scrutiny, because our allies had no such rule. The British do not have a shoot-first rule. Their ships in the Gulf prior to Earnest Will, as well as during Earnest Will, were operated under a much more restrictive philosophy, which was that they had to be fired upon before they could retaliate. When you're talking about an Exocet missile, you only need to get fired on once, and you may be in serious, serious trouble. It was a rule that I was very happy we were not under, and certainly the skippers of the ships were very pleased that they weren't under. It was something that at the bar with the Brits used to get discussed a good bit. Their skippers were very unhappy about that rule.

Paul Stillwell: Well, I talked to some of the skippers in the period between the *Stark* and the *Vincennes* incidents, and they had the feeling that had they had the opportunity to shoot, that they would be backed up for defending their ships.

Admiral Bernsen: That's right. Now, would I say that there wasn't more emphasis as a result of *Stark*? Hell, yes. I mean, when you promulgate rules of engagement and they're promulgated not as a result of an incident but simply as a prudent way of doing business, they tend to be taken for granted. When you do have an incident and it entails considerable loss of life and the destruction of a ship, people get a little bit more attuned to what's in those rules. But I don't want to make too much of that. The rules were the rules, and they were there, and they were briefed, and they were drilled. They were drilled for weeks and months before the ship ever arrived in the Gulf. The rules of engagement were promulgated to the ship back in CONUS during exercise workups for the cruise to the Gulf.* They had not only the exercise workups but the entire transit to go over and over and over those rules. Most wardrooms—I'd say virtually all of the wardrooms, literally every day would have question-and-answer sessions in the wardroom among all of the CIC officers, all the watch standers describing a situation and

---

* CONUS – Continental United States.

asking for a response. By the end of '87 there were all kinds of these scenarios that were promulgated. Literally handbooks. When you'd open it up, there would be scenarios and a bunch of questions. You would have a team leader, and he'd ask all the players what they were supposed to do.

By the time the ship got to the Gulf, my staff would conduct a test. They went on board the ship outside the Strait of Hormuz, usually off Fujairah at anchor. The guys would go out there in a small group, take the boat out, get on board, go down to the wardroom. They'd have quiz time and grade the ship, and they would come back and tell me. I would get a report on every one of those. "This ship is ready," or "This ship has got some serious problems," or something in between. If it had some serious problems, normally what then would happen was that the ops boss and whoever went down there, and usually it was the ops boss, would write up a message for my release. In many cases it was a personal from me to the skipper that said, "You know, my staff came aboard and you're a little weak here, you're a little weak there, you need to do some boning up here." But by and large it didn't take very long after the *Stark* incident before everybody was scoring 100%. But, again, the rules didn't really change. I mean, perhaps the President's emphasis was different, and I think they modified a couple of words in the actual guidance regarding the "shoot-down," but, in fact, as I stated earlier, that authority was already there.

Paul Stillwell: Well, the other part of it, though, was that the Iraqis were brought into the process more actively, so that they had an obligation to communicate because it was in their self-interest to do so.

Admiral Bernsen: Well, you've raised another completely separate issue but one that's certainly important, and that I was brought into. The thought there was that we would send a group of military officers to Baghdad to talk with counterpart military officers in the Iraqi armed forces, principally air force, and they would literally sit down and hammer out a deconfliction regime that we both could live by. The guy who headed up the team was David Rogers.[*]

---

[*] Rear Admiral David N. Rogers, USN, Deputy Director, Current Operations, J-3, Joint Chiefs of Staff.

Dave came out and visited me first on his way to Baghdad. He and the people that he had with him sat down with me and our staff, and they went through all of our concerns: "You know, this is something you can negotiate on; this is something we've got to be really hard line on. You can't negotiate on that point and so forth and so on." So I felt very good about that. I would have been extremely upset had this guy simply flown from Washington and bypassed go and gone to Baghdad, negotiated a whole set of rules that I was then or my forces were then going to have to live by. That didn't happen, and that in fact was the one period of time during which there were some direct calls to Baghdad. Not to the Iraqis but to Rogers. I think he had an office at the embassy while he was there. He and I talked on the phone, because he would go into the negotiation, the Iraqis would put something on the table, then he'd call me back and say, "How's that sound? Can you live with that?"

We'd mull it over for a while, and I'd say, "Yeah, I guess we can live with that." I'd get a few guys together, not a big formal drill, but we'd go through it, and I'd say, "Yeah, I think so." Or, "No, you'd better be pretty tough on that one because it's not a very good idea." He managed to come to grips with the deconfliction problem and worked out a set of pretty good rules. We did not have another *Stark* incident. Nor did we have any Iraqi airplanes shot down. Did we have some close calls later on? Yes, we did. I don't remember them in detail, but the system worked. It's one of the many factors in retrospect, after all of these years, that contributes to my feeling, and this is not 100%, but my overall general belief that the *Stark* incident was an accident and was not on purpose, because all of the things that we've seen indicate that that guy really was not briefed to go out and shoot the *Stark*. He just screwed up.

Paul Stillwell: Another thing that might have led him to believe that it was not a U. S. ship was that he didn't get illuminated. He might have expected that he would if it was a U.S. Navy ship.

Admiral Bernsen: I think you've put your finger on a very good point. I think that's absolutely true and the fact that nothing happened to him like happened a few nights earlier with the *Coontz* may have caused him to believe the coast was clear. I'm sure he must have talked to his buddy who went out previously. They all flew from the same base. Same type of airplane. Same mission. In fact, I suspect, although we don't know this, that the number of Iraqi pilots who actually did that mission was relatively few. Probably a half dozen or maybe at the most a dozen guys. Specially trained to do that mission, and you can't tell me that they all didn't talk to each other, probably every day. Briefed each other. So this guy, you're probably right, he expected that to happen. Probably would have done the same thing. We certainly would have expected that he would have done the same thing, turn around and go home. But he didn't get the signal.

Paul Stillwell: And another thing we could raise is a what if. What if there had been similar reciprocal conversations with the Iranians? It could have prevented the Airbus disaster.

Admiral Bernsen: I think you have point there as well. Just to put a fine point on this whole Iraqi situation, I had heard and read in the press about the assistance that the United States Government was providing Iraq in terms of photography, threat warning, just general information on Iranian military disposition, etc. I don't think I ever had any official correspondence on the subject. In fact. I'm 99% sure I didn't.

Paul Stillwell: Well, I heard there was also some guidance on how to harden targets to make them less vulnerable.

Admiral Bernsen: Well, there again, but I was never informed about that in either an official or an unofficial way, but what occurred to me very early on, even before the *Stark* incident but certainly was brought home even more after the *Stark* incident, was despite the fact that I was extremely upset over the *Stark* incident—that one thing, it would not serve me or anyone else to take sides in this Iran-Iraq situation. I frankly didn't like either side. I'd met some Iraqis I was not terribly fond of at the time. I felt they were rather supercilious and didn't hold us in very high regard. And, quite frankly. my study of Saddam Hussein, although rudimentary by standards today since we know so much more about him, I was well aware of the fact that he was a dictator. I was well aware of the fact that he had done some very nasty things. If you remember, I was the J-5 at CentCom.

Paul Stillwell: Right.

Admiral Bernsen: That was during the time when he gassed the Kurds in that village, so I mean I was aware, totally aware, this guy was a very nasty fellow.* So I was not about to come up at some press conference or in a one-on-one and say, "Boy oh boy, do we support the Iraqis. These guys are really neat, and the Iranians are all the bad guys." My pitch right down the line, and I don't think I varied, was that, "We are neutral. We are here to insure that a war between two protagonists does not spill over onto the Saudi Arabian Peninsula and that as a result the oil lifeline is jeopardized or that the war becomes a wider conflagration, other than involving those two countries." That was our mission. Stability. Keeping a lid on the situation. Not allowing it to grow.

Now, of course, we were roundly criticized frequently, because when once we had our escort mission going, the Iranians began to attack more ships, and the Iraqis were attacking more Iranian ships, so it looked as though our actions, if you assumed a cause-and-effect relationship, were causing this escalation in Iranian and in Iraqi activity. I never believed that. I truly didn't. I don't think it was our action that caused it. I think it was a natural progression of their own war. The Iraqis were getting more and more upset over the fact that the Iranians were still earning foreign currency by selling oil. They couldn't, because their export islands in the northern Gulf had been destroyed, so they couldn't go out in the Gulf without being attacked by the Iranians, so they were going to get back at them. And they were also going to get back at any neutral carriers that were carrying Iranian oil, and conversely the Iranians didn't want any supplies to get to Iraq. They were well aware that ships were coming into the Gulf, not American ships but other ships, that were delivering Russian tanks and guns to Kuwait and that they were going right off those ships onto the road right to Baghdad. So we had a situation that by its very nature was going to escalate regardless of what the hell the United States did. So my whole purpose whenever queried was to say, "We're not in the business of taking sides

---

* Hussein's minions used chemical agents against the Kurdish city of Halabja on 16 March 1988

here." I got cross-threaded a little bit with a couple of folks that came out of Washington who said, "What are you talking about? We really are—"

Paul Stillwell: Civilians? State Department?

Admiral Bernsen: Yes. "We really are taking sides because we're supporting the Iraqis against those bad, bad Iranians."

I said, "Well, maybe you are, but I don't officially know about that, and all I know about is what I see in the newspapers, and that's irrelevant to my mission. I'm not concerned about what you're doing in Baghdad." And, of course, later on I realized that we were doing a hell of a lot more than I was aware we were doing or that I thought we were doing. On the other hand, we also had our lovely Iran-Contra mission, so there were a number of things that were going on that weren't terribly helpful to me but that I really didn't have anything to do with and so was very loath to comment on.

Paul Stillwell: Well, having said all that about neutrality, still probably the stance with the individuals within the force was very much anti-Iranian, both because they posed a greater threat and because of the residue of the hostage crisis.

Admiral Bernsen: Yes. The gut feeling, the emotional feelings were certainly anti-Iranian. There's no question about that. But again primarily because until the *Stark* the Iraqis weren't a threat. At least nobody perceived them as a threat. And we didn't have a hostage crisis in Baghdad. I mean, let's face it, had Saddam Hussein been the guy dealing with the hostages, they might never have come back, as nasty as that fellow was. We didn't know anything about Saddam Hussein other than the little bit that I read about him and some background information that I had gotten. We didn't know very much about him. The average sailor didn't have a clue who the hell was running Iraq. It wasn't something anybody knew about.

Paul Stillwell: And not a high degree of sympathy for the Kurds.

Admiral Bernsen: No. The Kurds? Who are the Kurds? I mean, really. At CentCom the gassing of the Kurdish village was something that we were concerned about because it was in our AOR.* How many folks on the streets of the United States had even heard about it, much less were concerned about? Very few, so it wasn't something that was commonly known or accepted, and even if it had been I don't know that it was terribly meaningful to anybody. You're right. Who are the Kurds? Maybe they were so bad they deserved all that stuff like the PKK in Turkey. I don't know. Who knows?

But, anyway, we got through the *Stark* incident. We continued to march forward. and, of course, by July the first escort mission actually took place, the ships steamed north, *Bridgeton* in the van, and we had the famous incident when it struck a mine.

Paul Stillwell: I think you covered that pretty well last time. What you didn't cover as well was the reaction to the *Sea Isle City* being hit by the Silkworm.†

Admiral Bernsen: Okay. Well, that's certainly something that we've been reminded of here recently because of this World Court case. You have to understand the circumstances. When the *Sea Isle City* was struck by a Silkworm, the ship was parked in Kuwait City Harbor, just off the beach. The Iranians were occupying the Faw Peninsula, which was Iraqi territory about 40 miles northeast of Kuwait City. The Iranians had moved some Silkworm missiles onto the Faw Peninsula, and that's where these missiles were coming from. The Kuwaitis had put an observation team on a small island, Bubiyan Island, that they owned, which is partway in the direction of the Faw Peninsula. Those observation teams could clearly identify where the Silkworms were coming from. Those Silkworms are pretty obvious when they are launched. They're like our own missiles, like the famous pictures of downtown Baghdad, you could see those things.‡

Paul Stillwell: Roman candles.

---

* AOR – area of responsibility.
† On 16 October 1987 the re-flagged tanker *Sea Isle City* was at the Al-Ahmadi terminal in Kuwait when she was hit by an Iranian Silkworm missile. The ship's master, Captain John J. Hunt, was blinded by the explosion. The missile did extensive damage to the tanker.
‡ Out the outset of Desert Storm in January 1991, CNN carried televised coverage of long-range U.S. Tomahawk missiles hitting Baghdad and lighting up the night sky.

Admiral Bernsen: That's right. So, without much doubt, they weren't Iraqi missiles that were being fired. On that particular day the missiles were launched and homed in and struck the *Sea Isle City*. The skipper, who was American, was in fact injured seriously.

Paul Stillwell: Blinded, I think.

Admiral Bernsen: Correct. He was not killed but was blinded. And the ship was damaged. And since this was an American-flagged vessel, immediately, the policy question for not only me or not directly me but CentCom, DoD, Joint Chiefs of Staff, I suppose, Secretary of Defense, was, "What do we do? What kind of way do we demonstrate our displeasure?" A great many things were debated. One, of course, was, "Well, we'll just go in and we'll take out the town of Bandar Abbas, or we'll drop bombs on the Iranian naval base at Bandar Abbas, or we will take out some sort of a headquarters or we'll do whatever on the mainland of Iran." Another option, of course, was to go after the Silkworm missile site, which, of course, the next day was gone. Those rather radical solutions were—except for in some quarters—dismissed pretty much out of hand. No one in Washington in retrospect really was interested in an all-out attack on Iran.

Paul Stillwell: Were you queried as to any suggestions you might make?

Admiral Bernsen: Yes, I was, and at that time JTFME had been formed and was sitting out in the North Arabian Sea. Denny Brooks and his staff were queried. CentCom was working actively on a whole series of targets, but the real work was being done at JCS. JCS was tasked to come up with this list of options but asked for lots of input. I remember getting my staff together. We sat around and discussed all the various options that we could come up with. One of the ones that we came up with—I don't remember if it specifically was at that meeting, but it was to destroy or attack one of the installations that were in the Persian Gulf that were obviously Iranian. Farsi Island, of course, was one that particularly interested me, because that's where the boats had come from that laid the mines that hit the *Bridgeton*. I've never really forgiven the Iranians for that anyway, so that was an option, but Farsi Island wasn't really a very good option in Washington's opinion, I think because it was actually a piece of Iranian territory. But one of the things that certainly was discussed was the Rostam oil platform. There were a number of other oil platforms at Sirri and various places that in our view all supported some kind of Iranian observation or surveillance capability.

Paul Stillwell: How were you aware of what contribution that platform made to the military operation?

Admiral Bernsen: Well, we had a good many of those visual reports from the tanker captains even then, but we also had a considerable amount of communications activity that was sourced to the platforms, in my view, that was incontrovertible evidence.

Paul Stillwell: And you had CTs on board the flagship.[*]

Admiral Bernsen: And all of whom spoke Farsi and all of rest of it. I mean, there wasn't any doubt about that. Interestingly enough, way back in 1980 when two Iranian F-4s came in very low over the USS *La Salle*, that had all been directed from that same Rostam platform and that long time ago.[†] But, anyway, once we were queried and provided some suggestions, we were out of the loop. We really were. It became a CentCom-Washington exercise, and the decisions were obviously made there. The next thing I knew, we had a directive that said we were going to steam X number of ships to the Rostam oil platform. We were going to take up a position, and positions were even specific. There were very precise rules of engagement in this one. So many thousand yards, blah-blah-blah, and the folks on the platform were to be warned. They would be given, I think, it was 30 minutes to get off lock, stock and barrel, get out of there. At the end of that 30 minutes we were directed to put some folks on board to gather up whatever intelligence material they could find, and as soon as they got off, adios. We were going to blow that thing up.

---

[*] CT – communication technician, an enlisted rating.
[†] The F4H Phantom II was a jet fighter built by McDonnell. It first entered U.S. fleet squadrons in 1961. In 1962 the aircraft was redesignated F-4.

Paul Stillwell: Were you given any opportunity to critique the plan?

Admiral Bernsen: Well, what I'm going to tell you next will explain the situation in that respect. As I recall, most of the material directives, pieces of paper, that flowed out within the first 24-hour period, came to me or at least came to me as info. They had to go from CentCom to JTF, to Brooks out in the North Arabian Sea, but I was info on everything. What became also very clear to me was that Brooks was responding to these messages, and I wasn't being infoed until, quite frankly, I was told on the radio, by him personally, that I was not going to be involved. He was going to take this particular mission and execute it, and for purposes of executing the mission he was going to transfer from his flagship, which at the time I think was the cruiser *Long Beach*, over to a small boy. He was going to go in through the Strait of Hormuz into the Arabian Gulf, my command area, and deal with the Rostam oil platform, and then he would leave again. I was directed to take two of my ships and transfer tactical command to him. Plus later on a number of other folks were asked for specifically, either individuals or teams, particularly SEALs because we had a lot of SEALs assigned to us, and they were the guys that were going to be sent onto the platform before it was destroyed to dig out whatever kind of intelligence information they could find.

Paul Stillwell: They were also transferred to his command?

Admiral Bernsen: They were also transferred to his command. Now, he was in charge. He designated one of the skippers to be the surface warfare commander, who was actually the tactical commander, but Brooks was sitting there, and Brooks was inside the Gulf. I was not pleased.

Paul Stillwell: Understandably.

Admiral Bernsen: And I went through some very personal soul-searching trying to decide what to do about all this, if anything.

Paul Stillwell: I take it he was not directed to do this by CentCom. He took it on his own.

Admiral Bernsen: He took it on his own. I am absolutely sure, absolutely positive, that no one up the chain of command above him thought that anybody was going to carry out this operation other than the Middle East Force Commander in the Gulf, who was in fact assigned the mission in the Gulf. While we might get some staff support from Admiral Brooks and his folks, the mission accomplishment was going to be our staff's tasking. I've never met anybody who thought otherwise. Nobody even considered it. But a decision was made at CentCom not to countermand Brooks's assumption of the mission. When he came back and said, "This is my baby," nobody said, "No." They simply acquiesced. So I was left in the position of what do I do? And I'll be very honest with you. My decision was finally to just keep my mouth shut. In retrospect I think it was a good decision.

Paul Stillwell: What other options did you consider?

Admiral Bernsen: My options were a behind-the-back personal to General Crist, whom I knew 50 times better personally then Brooks did, of course, having worked for him as his J-5 and all the rest. But I really thought that there wasn't any way to put it on paper that didn't sound like sour grapes. There wasn't any way to put it on paper that didn't sound like I was trying to go around my boss, and at that point in time, which was very soon after Brooks had come to the Gulf. I was still not convinced that we couldn't get along reasonably well and get on with the program. That changed significantly later on, but at that point in time I felt that way, so I just kept my mouth shut.

We provided the forces that were requested, willingly and quickly, directed that the ships be detached, go do their thing, and of course we monitored all the frequencies as the exercise took place. He did info his subordinate. The Navy captain who was the tactical commander infoed us on all the traffic. I'm not sure I still got everything that came out of JTF, but we were well enough informed that we had a pretty good idea what was going on. Frankly, if he hadn't kept us reasonably well informed, I think he would have been extremely imprudent. That would have been a miscarriage, because obviously I had other ships in the Gulf, and if the Iranians had responded strongly to what we did, my forces could then have been in considerable danger.

I'll be honest with you. Getting away from the personal emotional aspect of this, the one thing that concerned me tactically, professionally, was here I had a guy in the Gulf who was not all that familiar with what was literally going on on the ground, on the water. He would be executing a mission in which nobody knew what the Iranians' reaction was going to be to this. We didn't know if they were going to fly 25 F-4s out and try and blow us out of the water. Had no clue. Under those circumstances it seemed to me that it would have been far better to have a single commander who was aware of all of the situation and could respond appropriately rather than to have two disparate commands less than 200 miles apart with one of them, namely me, not having the whole picture. That bothered the hell out of my ops officer, Dave Grieve. He was very unhappy about this, and I don't know that I can actually say this with certainty, but I have a feeling that he would have been very happy if I had been a bit more aggressive up the line.

Anyway, that was the situation, and it was done according to plan. The announcement was made. Everybody on the platform, all the Iranians, got off. The special warfare folks got on and picked up a pile of stuff, and then shortly thereafter they began firing, the ships, U.S. vessels began firing.* It was all 5-inch rounds, as far as I remember. The total number approached 1,100 rounds—1,065 rounds of 5-inch ammunition.

Paul Stillwell: That's a lot of bullets.

Admiral Bernsen: Oh, Jesus. A tremendous number of bullets. Now, what happened illustrates the difficulty in dealing with oil platforms. An awful lot of those bullets went underneath the structure, the building that housed the folks, and missed the pilings, just

---

* The bombardment of the Rostam complex was dubbed Operation Nimble Archer. It took place on 19 October 1987 and was executed by a surface action group that comprised the destroyers *Leftwich* (DD-984), *John Young* (DD-973), *Hoel* (DDG-13), and *Kidd* (DDG-993). Captain Isidore Larguier Jr., Commander Destroyer Squadron 35, embarked in the *Leftwich*, was the on-scene tactical commander.

went right by and out the other side. I think the really fortunate thing is that we didn't have ships in a big circle, or we'd have been shooting each other. But I don't mean to make light of this. They fired one hell of a lot of rounds, but the end result was that they destroyed the platform. It was a flaming hulk by the time it was finished, and I think there probably was a little letting off of steam here.

Paul Stillwell: A lot of enthusiasm.

Admiral Bernsen: A lot of enthusiasm. Absolutely. A tremendous amount of enthusiasm here. And finally after, I don't know, 20 minutes' worth of shooting like crazy, as fast as they could load and reload, the commander was queried as to the status of the platform. He said, "It's on fire, and it's really a mess." And the word came down directing them to cease fire. The ships that were assigned to me came back to me, and the rest of them steamed out of the Gulf.* End of story.

Paul Stillwell: Are there any ways in which it would have been differently executed had you been the operational commander?

Admiral Bernsen: I'll be honest with you. I don't know the answer to that. Because I didn't get the mission, probably in my pique, I just didn't spend a lot of time worrying about it. It was clear to me, even at that juncture from the conversations that I had had with Brooks, that had I provided some well-meaning advice it would have been disregarded anyway.

Paul Stillwell: And maybe counterproductive.

Admiral Bernsen: And maybe counterproductive. So I simply decided and told my staff, "If you're asked for an opinion, give it. If you see something that is blatantly dangerous— and by see I mean, if you hear on the radio or see in messages that they're

---

* The *Kidd* was assigned to Middle East Force, as were the cruiser *Standley* (CG-32) and frigate *Thach* (FFG-43), which provided support roles in the operation but did not participate in the firing.

going to do something that is completely crazy, then let me know, and we'll try and deal with it constructively." Nobody saw anything. It was a reasonably professional—it was very professional. Now, here's the kicker. I got a letter from President Reagan personally, complimenting me on how that mission was accomplished.

Paul Stillwell: How ironic. [Laughter]

Admiral Bernsen: Obviously, nobody back in Washington had picked up on the fact that Brooks had taken over the mission. I still have that letter framed in my den, because it's the only letter that I ever got from the President. But that's what it says: "You and your folks did a terrific job taking out that platform."

Paul Stillwell: What contingencies did you and/or Joint Task Force Middle East have in mind had the Iranians retaliated?

Admiral Bernsen: Well, I think that was the thing that was somewhat disturbing to me, because, really, there was no personal communication between Brooks and me. He didn't call me up on the phone and say, "Let's talk about what could happen." There wasn't any of that/. You prompted the answer, but you're absolutely correct. It was another thing that was of great concern not only to me but again to my operations officer and the rest of the staff was if the Iranians do something to retaliate, what the hell do we do? Well, the answer was we follow the rules of engagement as best we can and defend ourselves until we're told otherwise.

There are laws now. To the best of my knowledge, there was no contingency plan drawn up and agreed to by all of the players that said, "Okay, in the event there's a violent reaction on the part of Iran this is what we do." Now, Denny Brooks was not a stupid fellow. I mean, he happened not to like me, and we didn't get along. We disagreed on just about everything when it came to the Gulf and how to run it, but he was an aviator, fighter pilot, and I don't have any doubt he had some plan in mind. He had a carrier available out there, and certainly that carrier and the air wing were on very high alert. Had there been any reaction on the part of Iran, that's the tool that Brooks would have used. There's no doubt in my mind. Again, he was not a surface officer. I mean, yes, destroyers were fine to blow up the Rostam oil platform, but Denny Brooks was not relying on destroyers to take care of the Iranian situation. Yes, missile systems perhaps to shoot down an incoming, but the hammer, the retaliation, the tool which was clearly there to keep the Iranians from thinking about doing something bad was the carrier and the air wing. I have no doubt in my mind. At that point, by the way, I had no control over that carrier whatsoever.

Paul Stillwell: Well, that was out in the Gulf of Oman.

Admiral Bernsen: That's right, but I had had control of it before Brooks and JTF. Whenever we had an escort mission during the first two or three months of Earnest Will, when that escort mission entered what we arbitrarily set as the limits of the Strait of Hormuz till the convoy came back out again, the carrier was under my tactical command. In other words I could tell the carrier group commander, the other flag, even if he was senior to me—I could order him to launch.

Paul Stillwell: Were you a one-star at that point?

Admiral Bernsen: Yes. There were one-stars who were in command on those carriers, but they were probably more senior one-stars than I was. But I had that. That was part of the game plan here. Now, once JTF SWA came on the scene, Brooks was a two-star, though I don't know how senior he was at that point.[*] He'd come down from being CTF 77 in the Philippines.[†] That carrier came under his aegis, and in fact in the line diagram that carrier commander and the carrier group were I think at the same level I was, so we were parallel commands under JTF SWA, so if there was to be any retaliation or anything of that sort, I wasn't going to get involved in directing squat. It would have been the carrier and the carrier commander and the air wing that would have done the attacking, and basically what we would have done was damn well go into a defensive crouch.

---

[*] JTF SWA – Joint Task Force South West Asia.
[†] CTF 77 – Commander Task Force 77, the Seventh Fleet Carrier Force.

Paul Stillwell: Stay out of the way.

Admiral Bernsen: Stay the hell out of the way. Exactly. If somebody came flying overhead or threatened us, we would be at heightened alert. Well, certainly we would, and we already did this when the flagship was at sea. I wouldn't hang around the port of Manama because, of course, the Iranians obviously knew where the heck we were a good part of the time, and it was not a great idea to sit there at the pier under the circumstance. So we were away from the pier when all this occurred, as I recall.

Paul Stillwell: Well, that was before there was a solid consideration to send a battleship into the Gulf because of the feeling that quote unquote that would be provocative.

Admiral Bernsen: Yes. That's an interesting point, the great battleship debate. In this business about what's provocative and what isn't provocative, I think we tend as naval officers sometimes to be afflicted with something I call hubris. We tend to think that maybe some of the things that we do are perhaps a bit more important than they really are. Sending a battleship into the Gulf—as distinct from a destroyer or a cruiser or whatever—to the Iranians in my view meant absolutely nothing. I don't think they literally could figure out the difference other than the media may have been talking a battleship versus whatever. Now, sending an aircraft carrier into the Gulf, as we did during the Gulf War, I think that might have gotten somebody's attention. But sending a battleship in there, I don't think it was provocative. What it may have been to the less professional Iranian, who didn't know much about battleships, might have appeared to be a bigger target that they could attack and cause us pain, but there's an interesting story behind that.

Before the battleship did go in through the Strait of Hormuz, the Navy did some things in advance in preparation. The Navy turned on a group called SWEDG, which is a Surface Warfare Development Group right in Norfolk, to do an in-depth study of just what a Silkworm could accomplish against a battleship. They did a lot of work on thickness of armor plate versus warhead versus direct hits and non-direct hits, etc. And the head of SWEDG, who now is a very good friend of mine, was flown out to see me, as well as the skipper of the *Iowa*.

Paul Stillwell: Who was he?

Admiral Bernsen: Bob Powers is his name, a Navy captain at the time.* He now runs a think tank out here in Virginia Beach. He's actually a part of a bigger company up in Washington called Global Associates. He was flown out to me to brief me on just what could happen and how vulnerable the battleship was. Well, the studies and the various computer profile things that they had done indicated that the battleship could withstand a minimum of ten Silkworm hits, and I figured it was pretty unlikely for them to get hit ten times by a Silkworm. For that matter, if we got hit, if they fired one, again we were going to start blasting the hell out of them, not only with the battleship's guns but we were going to have airplanes in there again. So while certainly there was possibility of damage there was relatively little—nothing's positive in the world of warfare anyway—but there was relatively little chance that we were going to sink the battleship. That we were going to lose 1,800 sailors or however many they have in the crew that that wasn't really going to happen, particularly if we carried out a transit the way in which we ended up doing it, which, as you know, was to go through the strait fast as hell in the middle of the night. The chances of the Iranians being able to cope with that in any meaningful way were very slim.

Paul Stillwell: Well, we haven't discussed this specifically, but that's when the convoys went through the strait itself.

Admiral Bernsen: So, the battleship, however, was an interesting drill, and what also is interesting is that the skipper of that particular battleship at that particular time was right out here at the USNI Conference yesterday and the day before. His name is Bill Fogarty, and I can remember Bill Fogarty. He now works for FMC. I'm pretty sure that Fogarty was the guy at that time.

---

* Captain Robert C. Powers, USN.

Paul Stillwell: He had been relieved by then.*

Admiral Bernsen: Had he? Okay. I never personally met on scene the skipper of the battleship at the time. We never came in contact, but I knew that Fogarty was out there at the time, so, you're probably right.† I am terrible on ship captains' names.

Paul Stillwell: Al Carney had the *Missouri* in the fall of '87, and then Larry Seaquist came out with the *Iowa*.‡

Admiral Bernsen: Okay. Seaquist. Of course, Larry. That's right. That's it. That's right. Okay.

Paul Stillwell: One of the things you told me six months before the *Vincennes* incident was that you didn't need Aegis cruisers as part of your force. Why was that?

Admiral Bernsen: Well, I'm not sure why that was, frankly. That's a terrible thing to say. I'm trying to think.

Paul Stillwell: Well, they didn't come into the Gulf until after you left.

Admiral Bernsen: Well, I think the comment was made that I didn't need Aegis cruisers there.§ The comment was not that I was against Aegis cruisers. That wasn't the point or that I didn't think it was appropriate for Aegis cruisers. Aegis cruisers obviously were optimized to be the carrier defense, long-range interception of aircraft, etc., etc. In the context of what we were doing in the Gulf, I'm not sure that that was something that was necessary. Having said that, as this thing got more and more confrontational with the

---

* Captain William M. Fogarty, USN, commanded the battleship *New Jersey* (BB-62) from 28 December 1982 to 15 September 1983.
† In 1987, Fogarty, by then a rear admiral, was Commander Amphibious Group Two.
‡ Captain James A. Carney, USN, commanded the *Missouri* (BB-63) from 20 June 1986 to 6 July 1988. Captain Larry Seaquist, USN, commanded the *Iowa* (BB-61) from July 1986 to May 1988.
§ The Aegis air defense system, which involves the use of computers and phased-array radars, is installed in the cruisers of the *Ticonderoga* (CG-47) class and destroyers of the *Arleigh Burke* (DDG-51) class.

Iranians, and we began protecting neutral ships, not just American flag ships, I think it became the Navy's position that we were going to put in there whatever super-duper weapon system we had.

Paul Stillwell: That was the biggest game in town.

Admiral Bernsen: Biggest game in town and it did have with its SPY-1 radar an overland capability of sorts, and that maybe it would give you just a little bit more in-depth protection in the event the Iranians wanted to fly offshore and attack our ships, I don't know that I can argue with that. Again, earlier, I don't know that it was all that significant. And then maybe I was wrong when I said that. It may have been a slip.

Paul Stillwell: Well, you had some of the old CGs, the *Leahy* and *Belknap* classes with their NTDS systems.[*]

Admiral Bernsen: And, of course, they were double-enders too.[†] You know, in total numbers of missiles there were actually more missiles on some of those ships. On the other hand, I certainly wouldn't want to be quoted as saying that I thought those ships were more effective in the antiair role than an Aegis. That would be foolish and incorrect. I think when you're talking about the overall capability of the Aegis system, and being an E-2 pilot, I'm reasonably familiar with early warning and detection and that sort of thing.[‡] I think the fixed-array radar in the Aegis was really a far better system than anything else we had out there. But on any given day, who knows? Now, wait a minute. You remember we talked about ducting, and I'm wondering whether the Aegis, and I don't remember this, I truly do not remember, we did a lot of looking at, examining of which radars performed best under certain atmospheric conditions out there. Perhaps

---

[*] NTDS – Naval Tactical Data System, an electronic system that tracked radar contacts automatically, whereas previous practice had involved manual tracking. NTDS first entered the fleet in 1961.
[†] The *Leahy* (CG-16), class cruisers were double-enders with antiaircraft missile launchers forward and aft. The succeeding *Belknap* (CG-26) class had missile launchers forward and guns aft.
[‡] The E-2 Hawkeye is a propeller-driven carrier plane that has a look-down radar in order to track and manage the air picture from aloft.

the Aegis had a little bit of a problem, but I don't think so. I think the problems were far more prevalent with the conventional radars than with the Aegis SPY-1.

Paul Stillwell: Well, it could be also that you didn't expect the air threat to be so intense that you needed that much capability.

Admiral Bernsen: Could be. The Iranians never flew large numbers of groups of aircraft out over the Gulf. Normally when they were using F-4s, for example, to attack ships it would be one or two airplanes. A section. That's it. They obviously had more than that. Now, there were always questions as to their maintenance and how many they could get in the air at one time, but I guarantee you they could fly more than two. They didn't do that and I've always wondered about that. I don't know why they didn't. I suppose they may have had some commander said, "Gee, we don't want to be too provocative." You know, that's certainly possible. It's certainly possible. I really wouldn't want to conjecture. I don't know. But in fact they did not as a general rule fly large numbers of airplanes out over the water. Now, they had their own exercises up in central Iran and other places but not over the Gulf. Had they flown eight or ten F-4s out over the Gulf at one time, I think we would have been considerably more concerned about that.

Paul Stillwell: And probably beefed up the capability accordingly.

Admiral Bernsen: Yes. Right. We had AWACS, and operating the AWACS in and of itself was a very interesting drill. Positioning the AWACS became a topic of much conversation because we had U.S. Air Force folks, and we had various and sundry political restrictions in some cases, certainly in the political context, which said, "Where do you fly AWACS? Do you fly AWACS over northwestern Saudi Arabia or northeastern Saudi Arabia in that part of the Gulf, or would it be better if you flew AWACS down across the border between Saudi and the U.A.E., and if you do that can you get the agreement of both the Saudi and the U.A.E. Government to overlap the two countries and what kind of a relationship is that?"*

---

* U.A.E. – United Arab Emirates.

The U.A.E. wasn't totally different from today. The U.A.E. wasn't terribly anxious to be perceived by the Iranians as allowing U.S. to be fly in their airspace. Wasn't something they were interested in—not on a regular day-to-day non-threatening basis. So, let's face it, if we were most concerned about what was going on in the Strait of Hormuz it would have been a very nice additive if we could have had constant AWACS coverage over central U.A.E., and we could have really seen what was going on out there. In addition, of course, the E-2s were flying off the carriers, but nevertheless the AWACS would have been a very nice addition, but that wasn't part of the game. Politically it wasn't acceptable.

Paul Stillwell: Were there any political difficulties on where to base the AWACS planes?

Admiral Bernsen: Well, the AWACS deployment was always presumed to be in Saudi Arabia, and there were a number of reasons for that, not the least of which was that the Saudis were buying AWACS, so there was some synergy there, supposedly some training and various other things that were going to go on. The airfields in Saudi Arabia, the specific airfield which was in central Riyadh, where the AWACS flew from, had huge runways, all kinds of space for AWACS-type airplanes to fly from. That wasn't always true in other places.

Paul Stillwell: Well, I wonder if they were skittish politically about supporting the U.S. effort.

Admiral Bernsen: They may have been. But certainly CentCom sorted that one out, with State Department assistance. I mean, it was clear that the U.S.-operated, U.S.-manned AWACS that were flying out of Saudi bases were there to support the naval force, and the Saudis agreed to that. The Saudis weren't doing the actual flying. That was our bag. We were supporting our own people, but they were going to let us use their facilities— much like today. The Saudis don't fly in southern Iraq. The coalition, namely, the U.K., U.S., French, fly in Southern Watch, but there aren't any Saudi airplanes that fly in southern Iraq.* That's one of those things I'm not sure the American public either knows or cares about but it's true, they don't.

Paul Stillwell: I don't think they monitor that too closely.

Admiral Bernsen: No, they don't. We do that, but that's not a Saudi thing. They don't do that. We don't know why. But as the deployment of the AWACS dragged on, more and more imaginative ways of employing the AWACS became common, and in fact it did eventually fly down close to the U.A.E. border and was very helpful. The Air Force did not have sufficient numbers of AWACS aircraft deployed. They couldn't cover all these places all the time, but if there was a particular exercise like the escort mission coming in through the strait, then the AWACS would move down into that area, at least much closer than normal, to try and help us out. All of this took time. Okay, the minute you raised the issue then, "Oh, my God. Can we do that? Is that politically acceptable? How many governments do we have to talk to? And blah, blah, blah." So it would be discussed and all the possible ramifications examined, and then eventually it would get done. In most cases it would get done. I don't remember, and as I told you before, I didn't read the whole of the previous interview. Did we ever talk about over-flying the U.A.E. with U.S. aircraft?

Paul Stillwell: No.

Admiral Bernsen: I think this would be a useful thing to talk about for a just a minute, because in addition to the free-fuel enterprise that we spent so much time on in the last interview, this particular one is rather fascinating in that it sheds some light on the attitudes of the Arabs at that time, and perhaps it even gives our policymakers a little food for thought for how it might be in the future.

As I've alluded to, the U.A.E. really wanted to stay out of the conflict between Iran and Iraq, out of the tanker escort mission, except when it would profit them. They

---

* Operation Southern Watch was run by Joint Task Force Southwest Asia to enforce a no-fly zone over part of Iraq from the end of the first Gulf War in 1991 to the beginning of the U.S. invasion of Iraq in 2003.

were not interested in antagonizing the Iranians. Trade out of Dubai, between Dubai and Bandar Abbas, was going on just as before. Dubai dry docks, three dry docks, with one of them being a million-ton capacity, which I think is either the largest in the world or one of the two or three largest, was profiting mightily from the tanker war. They were repairing all kinds of tankers that had holes in them as a result of either Iranian or Iraqi firing, and the flag on the stern didn't make any difference. They were repairing Iranians next to Norwegians and whatever.

Paul Stillwell: A ship is a ship.

Admiral Bernsen: A ship is a ship, and money is money, and you want your ship repaired you just come in here, and we'll fix you right up. Nobody in the U.A.E. wanted to jeopardize any of those kinds of business relationships, much less get into a big political contest with Iran. Unlike the situation certainly immediately after the Gulf War, at this particular time, this is '86-7-8, most people in the U.A.E. were not that convinced that the United States was really going to stay the course. Now, we were still being plagued by memories of the bug-out in Lebanon and Vietnam and all the rest. The general consensus among the people I spoke to in the U.A.E.—and I spoke to many of them in those days—was that, "If the Iranians really got nasty and one of your ships gets blown up, like another *Stark* incident, you guys are going to leave, bug out. When the *Stark* incident happened and we didn't leave, that did strengthen our position just a bit, and they thought, "Gee, maybe these guys are serious. They've taken a few casualties, and they haven't left yet."

Nevertheless, bottom line, they did not want to appear to be getting too close to us. They didn't want us to go away, because although they wanted to trade with Iran and do all the normal things, they weren't terribly interested in being left in a position where they had no leverage with the Iranians. They were perfectly happy to say to the Iranians, "Gee, wouldn't it be nice if those Americans left and everyone got their act back to normal?" And, of course, what they were saying to us was, "Gee, we really don't want you to go. But, having said that, there isn't a great deal that we can do to help you either." There we were. That's basically in a nutshell what I perceived to be the political situation.

During the planning phases for Operation Earnest Will, I got a query from General Crist, which I think had come from Admiral Crowe. It said, "We really have to start thinking about contingencies in the event the Iranians come out and try to attack one of your ships. We have a carrier out here, and we presume that the carrier's air wing would be available to fly into the Gulf and assist, but we really need to deal with the practical aspects of how that would be accomplished."

Paul Stillwell: This is when you talked to Admiral Bull?

Admiral Bernsen: That's right, and we went through all of the carrier-related procedures, but I'm not going to get into all that again. That's not the point. The point here is we had a political situation that was a difficult one to sort out, because the quickest way to get from the carrier into anyplace in the Gulf was directly across the United Arab Emirates. This would not be winding around through some imaginary airspace ten miles wide in the Strait of Hormuz. It was straight across the U.A.E. Peninsula. I'm pretty sure that Bill Crowe and I probably talked about this issue. Certainly General Crist and I talked about it.

At the time I mentioned that I had met the Dubai military commander. He is Sheikh Mohammed, the second son of the former ruler of Dubai, Sheikh Rashid, who is now dead; in the federal organization of that country Sheikh Mohammed is nominally the Defense Minister.* Now, Abu Dhabi, because it has so much more money, actually controls the federated armed forces of the country, but interestingly enough there is an air base at Dubai, and Sheik Mohammed controls that air base. The airplanes and the helicopters that fly out of it actually belong to his own little force. They don't belong to the federated force. But he does have some radar capability. Did in those days. Not very sophisticated.

---

* Sheik Mohammed bin Rashid Al Maktoum has been Prime Minister of the United Arab Emirates since February 2006.

But the thing that he had was enough capability to detect a large force of airplanes coming toward the coast, maybe. Not absolutely sure he could do that, but I think probably. He could launch a few airplanes, which we honestly didn't think that he would ever do, but what he could do and might very well do was raise hell verbally, bring in the press, do the whole thing. "Who are these Americans flying airplanes over our sovereign airspace? No permission. No nothing. They just come in here and do these kinds of things." And the State Department types were scared to death that that's exactly what he would have done. So I was asked to go down to Dubai, where we have a consul general—our ambassador is in Abu Dhabi, a couple of hours away by car—and see if I could get a meeting with Sheikh Mohammed and raise the issue.

Paul Stillwell: Was this in the spring of '87?

Admiral Bernsen: Yes. And without a hell of a lot of guidance beyond that, I trundled down to U.A.E. I talked to the ambassador, gave him a little idea of what I thought I was going to say. He wasn't too sure if any of it made sense at all, and he had been told not to be part of this meeting. Didn't want it to be official in any way. Just wanted to be two military commanders talking to each other, even though one of them was wearing a dish-dash and has far more interest in racing horses than he does in flying airplanes or anything else, but I wasn't going to go over there all by myself. The guy who went with me was the CIA station chief who had met Sheikh Mohammed, and whom I knew, so it worked out very well. We contacted the correct hangers-on and made the appointment. It was carried out at his private athletic club that he has out in the desert, the interior of which looks precisely like some very, very beautiful English London club with the wainscoting and the dark mahogany walls and the whole thing.

Paul Stillwell: Leather chairs?

Admiral Bernsen: Leather chairs, the whole bit. Fake books in the bookcases and everything. I mean, it's absolutely incredible. You suddenly walk from the desert in through a door and a passageway, and here are you are in this totally air-conditioned area of no windows at all but a fireplace. The whole thing. And we had our chat. He was focusing on creating a golf course, which had not been built at that time, which is now the Dubai International Course. We talked a little bit about that and we talked about falcons. I can't remember what else we talked about.

Paul Stillwell: "Oh, by the way. Can we fly our airplanes over your country?"

Admiral Bernsen: As I recall, I did tell him about the escort mission when we met. He was very interested in that, because he'd heard about it, and he was appreciative of our efforts to help out the Kuwaitis. I think frankly that had a fair amount to do with the success of the visit. I told him about the mission and so forth and so on and how we were going to be escorting Kuwaiti ships with American flags into the Gulf. And I said, "You know, there could be an occasion when, due to an unforeseen incident, we might want to get some aircraft into the Gulf to support those ships." And I said, "You know, the one source of aircraft that we in the Navy have, that would be available, would be on an aircraft carrier out there in the North Arabian Sea."

"Oh, yes, of course," he said. "I understand that." Now, this guy was in his late 30s or early 40s.[*] I said, "There might be a situation where we would have to get aircraft in here as quickly as possible." And I really didn't know what I was going to say next.

He said, "Oooh, you mean a humanitarian mission." [Laughter]

I said, "Your Highness, you are absolutely correct. We might have a situation that would require some humanitarian assistance, aircraft humanitarian assistance."

He said, "I think it would be most appropriate if they flew directly over Dubai if they needed to do that to get there as quickly as possible."

I said, "You mean under those circumstances you wouldn't have any objections?"

"Of course not. We would be more than happy to acquiesce in this, and as a matter of fact, you don't even have to tell us about this. We would simply acknowledge the fact that if the airplanes came flying over the U.A.E. we would know that they had nothing to do with us, and they were embarked on a humanitarian mission."

---

[*] The sheikh was born 15 July 1949, so turned 38 in the summer of 1987.

Paul Stillwell: By definition.

Admiral Bernsen: By definition. We didn't have to make use of the "agreement" until after I left the Gulf in '88, and that was the *Roberts*. After the *Roberts*, when Tony Less engaged those two Iranian frigates you recall, and we sent aircraft from the air wing, and they flew right over the U.A.E.[*] And, just like Sheikh Mohammed said, nobody uttered a word. Not a peep.

Paul Stillwell: How could you argue against humanitarian efforts?

Admiral Bernsen: Can't argue against that, but I thought, and I will never forget, I remember the conversation so well, not because of what I said but because of the fact that he was so quick on the uptake, and I had run out of oblique ways of saying this. Obtuse ways. Next I was going to have to flat come out and say, "Look, we're going to fly some A-6s with bombs on them right over your city, and we don't want you to screw around with them."[†] But I didn't have to say that. We never ever got into that at all.

Paul Stillwell: I take it this whole discourse was in English.

Admiral Bernsen: Oh, yes. He's English educated. He speaks excellent English. This is the same fellow who has been on the cover of *Sports Illustrated* and in the papers for years. He's a horse lover and came to Kentucky and bought something like, I don't know, a $100 million worth of horseflesh. And he's the guy whose horses consistently win Epsom and the Derby and all the rest of it up there. And he sits in the Queen's box. I've seen pictures of him with a top hat and tails and the whole business. But he's a very, very smart guy, well educated, and has extraordinary presence.

---

[*] On 14 April 1988, the frigate *Samuel B. Roberts* (FFG-58) incurred extensive damage when she ran into and set off an Iranian naval mine in the central Persian Gulf. It took hours of effort on the part of the crew to save the ship from sinking. She received temporary repairs in Dubai and was later returned to the United States for rebuilding. For details see Bradley Peniston, *No Higher Honor: Saving the USS Samuel B. Roberts in the Persian Gulf* (Annapolis: Naval Institute Press, 2006).

[†] The Grumman-built A-6 Intruder was the Navy's principal carrier-based bomber from the early 1960s to the late 1990s.

Paul Stillwell: Marvelous story.

Admiral Bernsen: That's a true story, and that again, I think, shows how you can get things accomplished in the Gulf even today, even after the Gulf War. Some of them are almost by accident. In other words, the best-laid plans can go terribly awry, or in some cases things that appear to be much too hard can be accomplished very simply. I've been in the Gulf seven times in the last 12 months. My last visit was eight weeks during all of March, April and little bit of May in Bahrain and Dubai. I am convinced that the one common thread in all of this is the personal contact and relationship. We didn't have a lot of fax machines in '87, but there were ways to get a message through. Had I sent a message to Sheikh Mohammed, I probably would never have gotten a response of any kind. It would have been ignored. It would have gone into the round file.

Paul Stillwell: Because he didn't want anything on the record probably.

Admiral Bernsen: Absolutely. He was not going to write anything down and, of course, much of our bureaucracy will not function unless there is something in writing, in and out of the military but certainly within the military and the State Department. As you well know, ambassadors don't do anything unless it's in a cable. They are directed to do something. Thank God, we're not quite at that point in the military service yet, but I'm not convinced that we aren't reaching that. But certainly in the case of the Arabs you simply can't rely on doing business that way. You have to do it on a personal basis.

Now, subsequent to the war we've had huge problems in the U.A.E. We've shot ourselves in the foot, and they have been rather adamant in a few instances. You may recall the sailor incident in Dubai. He killed a child with his automobile and was put in jail. Of course, we raised all kinds of hell. Because of the Defense Cooperation Agreement we have with those folks, our government believed we should try the sailor and he should have been turned over. One of the strangest things about that really in a strange way was that the sailor turned out not to be an American citizen. He was a Liberian. He had not gotten his U.S. citizenship yet, but he was a uniformed sailor. Of course, the folks in the U.A.E. were not able to figure that one out, because we were raising a whole bunch of hell about their getting this American back, and it wasn't until the Navy finally raised its hand with the State Department and 'fessed up and said, "He really isn't an American." But that whole situation, and this has nothing to do with back in my time directly, but that whole situation in the U.A.E., without going into all the gory details, was not resolved until we changed Middle East Force Commanders. The folks who had been associated with the case on our side, it had reached such a hard-line position on both sides and had escalated to the very top that no reasonable decision could be reached without somebody losing face, at least in the view of the Emiratis.

Paul Stillwell: You mean the dead child drill?

Admiral Bernsen: The dead child drill. That's right. And the whole issue of jurisdiction. As a result, it wasn't until we had a new naval commander in the Gulf, who was not associated, at least in the Arab mind, with the other guy and the other things that were going on, was this negotiation able to resume. If we were ever going to get it taken care of, we almost had to replace the Secretary of Defense, and obviously we weren't going to do that, for that particular reason at least, because it had become a personal matter.

It always is a personal matter. There's always a personal dimension to these issues. Sheikh Mohammed, the oil thing, the free oil, the relationship that I had with the Emir in Bahrain, whatever it is, it is a personal relationship.* I see the Emir in Bahrain two to three times a year. I can honestly say that of all of the naval commanders who've been in the Gulf, perhaps with the exception of Bill Crowe, and I'm not really sure that's an exception, simply because of his status and stature and all the rest, I am the Emir's friend far more than any of the others, because the others left after their tour and I have been coming back for ten years, constantly. I'm a friend.

Secondly I was there during the Iran-Iraq period, which to the Emir of Bahrain was an unruly period internally. That was far more important and threat-critical to him than later on during the Iraq war when he knew that he had everybody in the world out there fighting for him, so it wasn't a big problem. Back during the '86-7 time frame the

---

* Sheikh Isa ibn Salman Al Khalifa was the first Emir of Bahrain; he served in that capacity from 2 November 1961 until his death on 6 March 1999.

Bahrainis weren't so sure that they had a whole bunch of folks out there ready to risk it for Bahrain. In addition to the ambassador, I was the only military guy who used to go in constantly, literally once a week, and tell him that we were covering his back, so to speak. We'd go through the drill and I'll give you one example because again I think it shows a purpose. It's the obliqueness, the way it works.

In 1972 the Brits withdrew from East of Suez, and the United States supposedly moved in to replace them but didn't. Our government was still extremely affected by the Vietnam situation. The Brits fully expected and indeed took three years of preparation to turn over the Gulf to us. And the position of the United States Government in those days was that the Shah of Iran and the rulers of Saudi Arabia would see to our interests, and we weren't going to be there. We had our one-ship Middle East Force. End of story.

At that time, when the Brits left Bahrain, the Bahrainian Emir, same guy, approached the United States via the U.S. naval commander (CMEF) who was in Bahrain, because we didn't have an ambassador there. He suggested that the United States and Bahrain come to an agreement similar to the one that the Bahrainis had with the Brits, which was that the Brits would in fact protect them. In fact, he was willing to cede foreign policy to us. I mean, he'd take care of everything in Bahrain as long as we took care of him and, of course, the United States Government said, "No way." We weren't going to do that.

Nevertheless, we would have a very warm relationship with Bahrain. We were certainly very happy and thankful that we were being provided some of their facilities, essentially the same facilities occupied by the British before us. But as far as a formal security pact, pledging that the United States would come to Bahrain's aid and rescue, we did not agree to that. We would pay rent for our facility, which we did. We paid a couple of million bucks every year. My supply officer used to carry a satchel over to the Bahraini Government bank. Anyway this particular relationship—remember, we've only got one Emir—many, many admirals. He, Sheikh Isa, remembers the whole continuum. He knows what he wants, but most of the admirals by 1986 weren't terribly interested in the political aspects and ramifications, so here I showed up in '86. As I mentioned, I had been there in '80 as skipper of the flagship *La Salle* and as CentCom J-5 and all these other things, so I've maybe got a little more background and have read a bit more than the average seaman apprentice about this situation, and I am aware that the position of the Bahraini Government, the expressed position, has been to encourage the United States to in fact create a closer security relationship. All right. That's the background.

So now we had this situation with Iran and Iraq fighting each other and we have Iranian airplanes flying up and down the Gulf attacking ships not very far away from Bahrain in many cases—40-50 miles sometimes. The Emir was aware of that. So were all of his folks, and he was totally aware that it would not be very difficult for one of those Iranian airplanes to stray, just like the *Stark* encounter but on the Iranian side, and come over and blow up his refinery. That was his sole source of income, by the way, other than handouts he got from the Saudis. Scared the shit out of him. So what he wanted was to have us state categorically that in the event such a thing might happen or be perceived to be a possibility that we'd protect him. We'd shoot down that Iranian airplane. That's what he wanted us to say, and he kept pressing me for this. And the first couple of times that he raised the issue, I just simply changed the subject, and we went on to something else.

Then one day I came up with a response. Never cleared it with anybody. Never told anybody about it. A couple of weeks later, I think I told the ambassador about it. I was in to see the Emir one day, and he started the same thing. "I'm very worried. I'm very concerned. The Iranians will come. They're training terrorists. Blah-blah-blah. We caught some. They're going to come and they'll blow up the refinery. What would you do about it?"

I said, "Your Highness, let me sort of walk you through a little scenario here. Now we are in a situation where in the harbor of Bahrain, at Manama, your harbor, we have at any given moment two to three warships," which was true. Usually more. I said, "Even though they are in the harbor, their systems are continually operating. The radars are on. They're detecting things. If one of those ships, under our rules of engagement, detects an Iranian aircraft coming toward Bahrain, our rules of engagement would have us do these things. We would warn them not to approach." I didn't give him the exact stuff but generally speaking. I said, "If they did not comply, we would shoot them down and not comply means that they didn't turn around and go away."

He looked at me, and he said, "You mean you would shoot them down if they were coming toward Bahrain, and they did not turn around if you told them to and you would tell them to?"

I said, "Absolutely. All of those things are correct. That's what we would do."

Well, he's only 5-feet-4, 5-3; he's a little teeny guy, and the look on his face was beatific. He said, "Oh, Admiral, that is so, so reassuring. That is so wonderful."

I said, "Well, that is in fact what we would do."

He said, "I have a request. Would you always keep at least one warship in my harbor?"

I said, "I'm going to try and do that." And the interesting thing is that we were able to do that, just about, certainly the entire rest of the time I was there, and the rest of the escort mission. I came back and talked to my ops boss. I didn't go through all this. I just said to Captain Grieve, "Dave, as much as you can. This is not a direct order or an absolute policy, but if it doesn't really conflict with your operational scheduling keep one combatant lit off in the harbor 24 hours a day.

Paul Stillwell: For humanitarian self-defense.

Admiral Bernsen: That's right. That's exactly right. Now, we never got into the business of what would happen if the ship were in the harbor in a neutral country. I mean, our rules of engagement really didn't go into all that stuff, but I gave him reassurance in a way that he understood perfectly, that was as close to the truth as it could be. The fact of the matter is that if an Iranian aircraft had flown across the Gulf and had been picked up by radar on the ship in the port, they would have queried them. And I can only assume that we would have shot them down if we needed to. [Chuckle] I'm reasonably convinced that ten years later, in 1997, ten years almost to the month, that when I go and visit Sheikh Isa that he still remembers that, and that it's one of the reasons—if not *the* reason—why I'm still his favorite admiral.

Paul Stillwell: Well, as a matter of expediency you were able to give him the thing he most wanted.

Admiral Bernsen: I wasn't violating any policy. Sure, it was a little bit phony, but on the other hand we needed that guy, and that last thing that I wanted to do was get Sheikh Isa upset with me. And for him, honestly, and this was really what was important, for him to believe for one minute that we really weren't committed to helping Bahrain in some meaningful way, I think if he really had believed down deep inside that we weren't willing to go to bat for him, our relationship might have been very different. At that point in time without Bahrain and ASU and the pier and the warehouses, and God knows what all, we couldn't function.* I don't think Earnest Will could conceivably have happened in the way in which it did without having Bahrain as a centerpiece of our communications, supply, and logistics effort.

Paul Stillwell: Could you talk a little, please, about what ASU contributed?

Admiral Bernsen: ASU, the administrative support unit, was a ten-acre parcel of land which had been part of the British Juffair naval base back during the long period of British tenure. When the Brits left, an agreement was reached between the United States Navy, United States Government—remember, there was no United States ambassador until the mid '70s. This was in the '70-'71 period. An agreement was reached that allowed us to have ten acres of that property. Now, we already had a ship there. That was the Middle East Force flagship that in most cases, as you recall, it was a small tender, tied up at the pier.† But we really didn't have any piece of land to call our own, but now we did, and that was ASU.

ASU was a sleepy little place, by and large, during the '70s and early '80s catering to the needs of the one or two U.S. ships that came into the port, commanded by a Navy commander when I showed up there. I think in '80 it was a commander as well, staffed by about 90 sailors. About 90 sailors. That's it. Some of those sailors were married, and they were allowed to have their families over there, strangely enough. ASU served as an R&R provider for the crews of visiting ships.‡ They had a small officers'

---

* ASU – administrative support unit, Manama, Bahrain.
† For many years, World War II-vintage small seaplane tenders, AVPs, rotated as the Middle East Force flagships.
‡ R&R – rest and recreation.

club, which was the old British officers' club, and a movie theater. There was a very large, lovely swimming pool. There was an enlisted club with food, nothing very fancy, but it was okay. Hamburgers, hot dogs, and that sort of thing. Pool tables, etc.

There was a post office, and that's where the force's mail was cycled through. It came in from the ships, collected by *La Salle*'s helicopter. We had a chaplain there. There was a small medical facility. There was a doctor there, because although a ship like *La Salle* had a doctor, the small boys didn't always have one. So there was a doctor there, a naval surgeon.

Paul Stillwell: And you had some warehouses for supplies.

Admiral Bernsen: Well, the reason I didn't mention them initially is because there weren't any warehouses initially. Warehouses were something that became a great subject of concern and debate about 1986-87. As we got more and more ships into the Gulf, and particularly when we brought the little minesweepers in '87 and when we brought in the SEALs and their small craft, all of a sudden we didn't have anywhere to put all of the stuff that was required to support all these folks. Where we put it was in the middle of this little ten-acre tract. There were little roads that connected the various buildings and such, and pallets began to accumulate in vertical stacks in the middle of these roads. You barely could see from one building to the next.

The place was incredible, and the skipper of ASU came to me and said he badly needed help, storage space, and more people. I mean, obviously I could see it every day. It got worse and worse and worse all through the spring of '87 until it was truly a disaster. We couldn't function. We were just not functioning. Nobody could keep track of anything, much less get it moving from one place to another. The ships were getting very frustrated. Now, most of their critical spare parts would come in by air and would be delivered directly from the small military facility we had at the civilian airport in Manama, right by helicopter out to the ship. But if they ever got into the ASU muddle, it might never get out of there. All the routine stuff like rags and oil and all the rest of it never got anywhere.

Anyway, long story short, we started negotiating with the Bahraini Government to get some warehouse space. There were lots of warehouses available, and eventually we signed a contract with the government and we rented, leased a warehouse I think owned, with a couple of middlemen, but I think ultimately owned by the Prime Minister. It was called Banz, B-A-N-Z, simply because that was the name of the chilled-food company that owned that particular set of warehouses. That was where we ended up putting all the stuff we couldn't fit into ASU. Once that initial contract was made, and that was the big deal here, we still had the problem of ASU and its small size.

Remember, it had been in existence for close to 15 years. Never gotten any bigger. Didn't get any smaller. It was totally stable. Everybody knew it was there. It was purposely not called a base. It was the Administrative Support Unit, and it didn't change, and we paid X amount of money to rent that, plus a pier space and for our little building that we had at the airbase. So we first went to the ambassador and suggested, "Geez, we need some more land."

"Oh, my God. Can't change it. Can't have any more. You've got to work with what you've got."

"Now wait a minute. Now we've done that. I've got 42 naval commands out here. It's impossible. We can't function this way. We must have more space. All of the to-ing and the fro-ing and, I mean, personal visits literally to the Foreign Minister and Prime Minister and everybody in between to outline in great detail exactly why I wanted to rent a warehouse. That was my job. And it was unbelievable. Sam Zakhem, our ambassador, was the first political appointee that had ever been assigned to Bahrain. He was born in Lebanon and spoke with a Lebanese accent but was an iconoclast of the first order. Buddy of Ed Meese, sent out there and thought the State Department were a bunch of fools.* But the thing was he was right-wing conservative, a little bit to the right of Attila the Hun, and anything that the admiral wanted, he figured that was fine with him. So he would get right behind me and we would go in and see all these officials and he would chime in and say, "The admiral needs that, no question about it, and I support it."

---

* Edwin Meese III served from 1981 to 1985 as counselor to the President and a member of the National Security Council. From 1985 to 1988 he was U.S. Attorney General.

The only problem with all that was that he never went back to the State Department and got any directive or clarification, so he got himself in all kinds of hot water. There were constantly cables coming out there that said, "We didn't tell you to do that, and you went and did it anyway. What's going on out there? Tell that admiral he can't do that." So there was a lot of that going on, but in the final analysis we got what we wanted, and little by little over that period of time ASU, while it didn't actually expand its perimeter it acquired things. Another building out at the airbase. More vehicles. Rented more warehouses. The long-term agreement stipulated that we could only come alongside the pier, one berth, X number of days a month.

By the time Earnest Will had gotten into high gear, why, we had two or three places at the pier, and we could be there all the time. Not only that, but we had minesweepers tied up there indefinitely literally. So a lot of the things and a lot of those restrictions that the embassy team and the admiral had scrupulously adhered to for all of those years so as not to irritate the Bahraini, so as not to make waves and destabilize the situation, simply went out the window. Once we got the warehouse and we had gone through that drill, then it was very easy, and the Bahrainis were right. I mean, whether it was the Foreign Minister, Prime Minister, or who it was—one of them informally said to me, "You know, once we agree to one of your requests, you know, I know we're going to get another 15." And, gee, he was right, because the minute we got one thing approved, we needed so much more, and he got more requests.

Paul Stillwell: But the logjam was broken by then.

Admiral Bernsen: That's right, and the Bahrainis acceded to the requests, so the State Department was not quite so concerned about what the reaction was going to be, whether it was going to be positive or negative.

Paul Stillwell: Well, but I wonder if their willingness was tied into your giving the assurance of defense.

Admiral Bernsen: No question about it. Had we not been perceived as being a very positive thing for them, there wouldn't have been any warehouses or anything. It would have been, "Well, we have to study it," or, "We'll get back to you," or "How does this affect the overall relationship, and what about the rents?" I mean, it would have been a million things, and it would have gone on for weeks and weeks and weeks, and we would have pulled out our hair. And, of course, Bahrain does depend on us to a degree and, you know, eventually probably we would have gotten what we wanted, but in this particular case it was not all that difficult. Once we greased the wheels and talked to the right folks, again, to make them feel like we really believed that they had the power and authority and, you know, we were coming to them. They were a sovereign country and we were coming to them to go through the motions. I suppose conceivably, George Crist or the Assistant Secretary of State could have come flying in and said, "Listen, fellows, that's it. You know, we don't want to hear any nonsense about this. This is what we want, and that's what we're going to get." And I don't know. The Bahrainis probably would have had not much choice. But that wasn't the way to do it. We didn't really want to do that. It was far better to get them to feel that they were contributing and also to make them understand how necessary it was.

Paul Stillwell: And in their self-interest.

Admiral Bernsen: In their self-interest. Absolutely.

Paul Stillwell: Well, you made the point that a lot of these actions depended on personal relationships, and the personal relationships depended on the United States having a continuous naval presence there for 40 years prior to that.

Admiral Bernsen: Bahrain is such a unique place, and the relationship is so unique, and it's even true today. Because the Navy had been there from '48 or '49 on, and we didn't get an ambassador till the mid-'70s. The Emir has all of that corporate knowledge going way back to when the only people he dealt with were the Navy and the Navy admirals. It's the only country in the world, I'm convinced of it, where the Emir himself considers the ambassador number two. [Chuckle] And if you don't think we've had a couple of ambassadors who have been very disturbed by that, you've got another think coming.

The funny part is that, of course, they've never been exposed to it before, so they come to the position assuming that this is like any other post in the world and as the ambassador therefore they are by definition the primo U.S. representative. The first time the ambassador gets called out to see the Emir, the Emir says, "You didn't bring the admiral today, Ambassador."

And the ambassador says, "No, I certainly didn't, and why in the hell would I?" You know, that's what he's thinking. And the Emir says during the conversation, "Well, maybe the next time you come you ought to bring the admiral if he's around." And it's really a very different point of view. Now, I don't want to overstate this, obviously. There are issues today after having an ambassador for over 20 years now which are clearly State Department ambassadorial things that the Emir, Prime Minister talk with them about. But about three years ago, during one of my visits I was having lunch with our ambassador, who was a very interesting guy who was also a political appointee and is no longer in the embassy, in the State Department service. As we were sitting at lunch, he had been there about two years and said, "You know, Hal, it's amazing. I was here for over a year and a half when the light finally came on, and I realized the guy that they really like around here is the admiral and not the ambassador."

I said, "Well, you're one of the few that I think have really understood that."

"Well," he said, "That's okay. I just play that. Clearly, it doesn't enter into every aspect of the relationship, but certainly it enters into many areas, and whenever we get talking about who's going to protect this island and all the rest of it, they don't believe me. I mean, I might as well talk myself blue in the face, but the admiral comes in here and gives them some stuff, they believe that. They go along with that."

Paul Stillwell: Good to have that kind of credibility.

Admiral Bernsen: It really is. It's amazing.

Paul Stillwell: You talked about the muddle there at Bahrain. Did the supply officer that Admiral Walker sent out help unscrew that muddle?

Admiral Bernsen: Oh, yes. Oh, yes. Oh, that's the unsung hero of the war. O-6. I saw Walker not very long ago, as a matter of fact. We reminisced a little bit about that. We always do. Walker perceived that we had a serious problem.

Paul Stillwell: Very correctly perceived it.

Admiral Bernsen: Yes, I mean really serious. And, as he's told me subsequently, a long time afterward, he said, "I went around and told a whole bunch of folks at OpNav about your problem. Nobody seemed to care enough to do anything about it. You know, I really went out on a limb. I just took it on myself to send you some help." And that's what he did. Now, truly on his own, without any OpNav direction he sent us Captain Mike Hoyt.[*] He was the O-6 who came out, presented himself smartly to me right away rather than secreting himself at ASU and whatever. He came right to me on the flagship, knocked on the door, and said, "Admiral, I present Admiral Walker's compliments, and I'm here to help you, and I really mean that. I'm going to take a look at ASU, and Admiral Walker wants to send out whatever you need."

I said, "Thank God." I was so operationally overcommitted that I hadn't time to think about how to deal with the problem. I mean, every day the problem was there but how to deal with it, and I had written a couple of messages about it. Basically I said to the ASU commander, "You know, you've got to deal with it. You go through your own chain of command and get some help." The problem was that I wasn't responsible for that place. The ASU commander did not report to me. He reported to a rear admiral in Hawaii, because that was the silly command thing that had been generated when CentCom came into being and took over the responsibility for the Gulf. The Navy admiral, who was ComUSNavCent, was Admiral Jesburg in Hawaii, and I was commander of Middle East Force. And on the line diagram I was subordinate to that guy in Hawaii, but it was only really in regard to logistics support. But that guy in Hawaii

---

[*] Captain Michael C. Hoyt, Supply Corps, USN.

wrote the fitness report of the commander of ASU. Can you believe that? I mean, it was a screwed-up mess.

Paul Stillwell: That's bizarre.

Admiral Bernsen: It was bizarre. Now, the skipper of ASU was a very smart guy. And he knew that the guy in Hawaii was a long way away, and I was very, very close by, so he was pretty good about making sure that I was cut into the loop, but the fact of the matter is the guy from Hawaii showed up every now and then. Fortunately, we got along pretty well. Ron Jesberg lives right here in Williamsburg, and I still see him. Phil Duffy was another one of the guys out there. There were others. But he would come out and do his inspections and do his admins and all that stuff. I didn't do any of that. Right away, Captain Hoyt went over there, because ASU was such a disaster. The supply officer at ASU was a lieutenant, and that was the standard organizational lash-up.

All of sudden, he had an O-6. The captain didn't actually take the job. He just was an advisor, if you will, a helper. But Hoyt organized it. I mean, he was good, and he was sharp, and he was dedicated, and things began to change right away. When we physically got the warehouse sorted out, and he succeeded in reorganizing the supply support, we then got an infusion of like—I can't give you an exact number, but I'm sure it was about 20 enlisted people who came out of the Navy supply organization somewhere and showed up TAD.

We didn't have any billets to which we could assign these guys, and nobody in OpNav was changing billets. Nobody was adding billets to ASU, and that leads to probably the last story of the day, but I'm going to tell you a short one. I'm going to tell a story on a boss of mine and a boss whom I happen to think a great deal of, Carl Trost.[*] The CNO came for a visit. When was it?

Paul Stillwell: It was the fall of '87, because that's when he helped get the MSC tanker situation straightened out.[†]

---

[*] Admiral Carlisle A. H. Trost, USN, was Chief of Naval Operations from 1 July 1986 to 29 June 1990.
[†] Admiral Trost visited the Persian Gulf/Arabian Sea area in November 1987.

Admiral Bernsen: That's exactly when it was. Same trip. Despite all of this help from the supply folks and the fact that we were organized now at ASU, and we didn't have any more piles of pallets and boxes in the street, the major problem that continued to plague us was mail. The way the skipper at ASU sorted this one out—and here we were totally together—is that one of the directives that went to every ship that came into the Middle East Force was to contribute one mail PO to ASU.[*] So every ship did. Now, that meant that we had a lot of mail POs. Now, what the ship sent under that rubric could be anything from Seaman Apprentice Jones to somebody who really knew something about the mail. We had a first class in charge. The guy who was the CO of ASU at that time was Commander Dale Brink.[†] Dale was laid back but a smart guy, so he had come to me before we found out Trost was coming, and, of course, everybody was figuring out what we were going to do with him. So old Dale had written up a list of things that he wanted to talk to the CNO about. All of them were in the logistic support area—all these bad things that he wanted to talk about.

I said, "Wait a minute, Dale. Let's pick out two or three things that are really significant, and we'll raise them. I'll let you raise them with the CNO. I want you to do this, but I'll support you. If we just give him a whole laundry list, you never accomplish much that way. Sure, he knows we've got problems." Anyway the CNO arrived, and one of the things we did, I guess the second morning he was there, was we gave him a tour of ASU. I said, "This supports me. I'm the operational commander, but I don't run the place. By persuasion I run it but not directly." And Gale was taking him on a tour, and very purposefully the mailroom was left to the end. Well, the mailroom consisted of this little house with sacks of mail spread in all directions, outdoors, outside the house, with half a dozen of these seamen and seaman apprentices running around moving mail from one place to the other and, of course, the Supply Corps lieutenant was in charge.

Dale said, "Come on out here, Petty Officer Jones and tell the CNO about the problem here." Petty Officer Jones did that. The CNO listened matter of factly, and Commander Brink said, "We don't have any billets, Admiral. There are no billets. These are just augmentees. They turn over almost every day. I've got to have some

---
[*] PO – petty officer.
[†] Commander Dale D. Brink, USN, a surface warfare officer.

permanent billets to support this operation. The number of billets was exactly the same when we had two ships in the Gulf as it is today."

Carl Trost turned around and looked me straight in the eye and said, "Hal, I think that maybe you ought to go back to CentCom, and maybe some of those 800 guys in that headquarters down at Tampa could be sent out here to take care of the mail problem." End of story.

Paul Stillwell: Let that not be the end. What happened after that?

Admiral Bernsen: We continued to deal with the problem just the way we he been doing. Obviously, I didn't go back to General Crist and tell him to send some of his headquarters personnel out to deal with our mail problem, but Trost did not deal with it.

Paul Stillwell: He didn't see it as his problem.

Admiral Bernsen: No. But, of course, it was his problem. It was the Navy's problem. It was not General Crist's problem. It was the Navy's problem. But Trost had gotten beaten up so badly. I mean, almost half the Navy was over there. Let's face it, this operation was Navy intensive. The Army wasn't hurting because of this thing. The CNO looked at this thing. Of course, Carl Trost is not a dummy; Carl Trost recognized that this was a mission, and it was important and the oil and Iran-Iraq War. But what he was seeing was a mission that was literally draining the Navy of countless billions of dollars to maintain. The numbers of ships involved, the disruptions of training cycles, to time at home, to budgets—

Paul Stillwell: Logistic support, fuel—

Admiral Bernsen: The whole nine yards, and I think his frustration stemmed from being the one guy who was beaten on constantly about supporting this drill over here without the Navy getting any add-ons. There was no big pile of money that came drifting over to the U.S. Navy to take care of this problem. Now, of course, we got the free fuel later, and that was all well and good, but still it was a problem. And I think what I saw that day was Carl Trost's utter frustration and the fact that you've got to really look under the tablecloth here because remember the whole business about CentCom taking over an AOR that had been exclusively CinCPac's and CinCLant's. You know, this was Navy, this thing here. Now, Navy was being run by a four-star something else. Now, at that time it happened to be a Marine, Crist, but just before that it was an Army four-star, and it was going to be an Army four-star directly after Crist. And the Navy wasn't running it, and Carl Trost never accepted that, nor did most of the other CNOs that I ever ran across. It just irked the living hell out of them, and the point was that this thing was screwed up. Let that guy down in Tampa figure out how to unscrew it and what are they doing with the 800 guys in that headquarters down there? Have you ever been to CentCom?

Paul Stillwell: No.

Admiral Bernsen: When it was conceived and the decision was made to put CentCom at MacDill Air Force Base, there wasn't any building available, they appropriated, I don't know, take a number out of the air, $20 million and built the headquarters. I mean, it is the only headquarters that I know of in the United States military that was built today, I mean in modern times, as a headquarters, with all of the appropriate walls X number of inches thick to protect against emissions and satellite pickup and the whole bit. It was organized and staffed differently. The other CinCs, like Pac in particular, had fewer people directly assigned. Over the years, as additional support was required, for example, intelligence or communications support, you established a small Navy or joint unit, gave it a name, gave it a commander, but you didn't directly attach it to the major staff. But what the hell was it doing out there? It was supporting the staff, right? But you didn't call it part of the staff. It was Fleet Intelligence or Fleet Communications or something similar. Well, down at CentCom they didn't do that. This was to be an ideally organized, 100% supportive, self-sufficient staff, so the staff was organized as an 800-man staff, and that number, considered huge by most standards, became the buzzword.

I don't know how many senior naval officers who were involved in trying to prevent CentCom from being established actually knew about the 800-man CentCom staff. But even though there were probably 1,200 guys in Hawaii or more supporting that CinCPac bunch, it was the 800 at CentCom that became the target, because you could define those bastards, right? They had a C in front of their name, and that's what it was, and I'll never forget it when Carl turned to me, and it was the 800-man staff. It was just beautiful. Of course, he knew full well when he turned to me that I had been there. I was part of that organization. Not that he held it against me personally.

Paul Stillwell: He thought you had sold your soul to this—

Admiral Bernsen: I'd sold my soul to that 800-man megalith down there that had taken the mission away from the United States Navy, and if it weren't for those guys down there we'd be running the show. And it was so beautiful. Of all of the comments that were ever made by a senior Navy flag officer, in its own way it was the most expressive. It summed up, for me anyway, the whole idea of why the Navy, while it stood up and saluted and went and did it and did all the war fighting, nobody ever complained about that. When it came to all the little nuts and bolts and the support and all of the rest of it, a lot of folks said, "Jesus Christ, why are we doing this and can't we get the hell out from under? And what about CentCom? They're not helping. They're just screwing it up."

Paul Stillwell: How nice for you that Admiral Walker didn't have that baggage.

Admiral Bernsen: It was wonderful. Admiral Walker—and we have talked about it face to face in years since. Admiral Walker just flat didn't care about any of that. He knew that sailors weren't getting the mail, and sailors weren't getting their supplies, and the rags weren't getting to the ships and folks were bitching and moaning, and he was there to fix it and he did and he did a great job. I'll be forever in his debt. He was superb.

Paul Stillwell: Well, Admiral, this is another great installment today. I look forward to the next one, whenever that happens to be.[*]

---

[*] Sadly, there were no further interviews in the series.

Launched in 1969, the U.S. Naval Institute's award-winning oral history program is among the oldest in the country. Used in combination with documentary sources, oral histories offer a richer understanding of naval history through candid recollections and explanations rarely entered into contemporary records. In addition, they help depict the atmosphere of a particular event or era in a manner not available in official documents.

The nonprofit Naval Institute accomplishes its history projects through contributed funds and gratefully accepts tax-deductible gifts of all sizes for this purpose. This support allows the Institute to preserve the life experiences of today's service men and women so they may enlighten and inspire future generations.

For information about opportunities to underwrite Naval Institute oral history projects, please contact the Naval Institute Foundation at 291 Wood Road, Annapolis, Maryland 21402; by phone at (410) 295-1054; or by e-mail at foundation@usni.org.

Index to the Oral History of
Rear Admiral Harold J. Bernsen, U.S. Navy (Retired)

Aegis System
   In 1987-88 Commander Middle East Force did not see the need for Aegis cruisers in the Persian Gulf, 107-109

Air Force, U.S.
   In May 1987 an E-3 Sentry tracked an Iraqi fighter headed toward the guided missile destroyer *Coontz* (DDG-40) in the Persian Gulf, 68
   In May 1987 an E-3 Sentry tracked an Iraqi fighter headed toward the guided missile frigate *Stark* (FFG-31) in the Persian Gulf, 71
   Use of AWACS during Operation Earnest Will in 1987-88, 109-111
   MacDill Air Force Base in Tampa is the site of the Central Command Headquarters, 132-133

Army, U.S.
   Support of Operation Earnest Will in the Persian Gulf in 1987-88, 19-20

AWACS
   In May 1987 a U.S. Air Force E-3 Sentry tracked an Iraqi fighter headed toward the guided missile destroyer *Coontz* (DDG-40) in the Persian Gulf, 68
   In May 1987 a U.S. Air Force E-3 Sentry tracked an Iraqi fighter headed toward the guided missile frigate *Stark* (FFG-31) in the Persian Gulf, 71
   Use of during Operation Earnest Will in 1987-88, 109-111

Bahrain
   In the 1970s and 1980s served as home base for the Middle East Force flagship *La Salle* (AGF-3), 4, 14, 67-71
   In 1972 the British withdrew from East of Suez, including Bahrain, where the U.S. Navy took over the Juffair naval base, 119, 122-123
   Site of the administrative support unit for the Middle East Force in the late 1980s, 39-40, 55-60, 119-130
   Location of a news conference following the attack on the guided missile frigate *Stark* (FFG-31) in 1987, 80-81
   Relied on the United States for protection in the late 1980s, 4, 118-122
   Sheikh Isa ibn Salman Al Khalifa, the Emir, had a personal relationship with Bernsen in the 1980s and 1990s, 118-122, 126-127

Bernsen, Rear Admiral Harold J., USN (Ret.)
   Commanded the Middle East Force flagship *La Salle* (AGF-3), 1980-82, 2, 98, 119
   In the mid-1980s was plans and policy chief for CentCom, 2, 6, 119
   Served as Commander Middle East Force, 1986-88, 1-134
   Deliberately did not take sides publicly in the Iran-Iraq tanker war, 93-96
   In 1988-80 served on the staff of Commander in Chief Atlantic Fleet, 62-63

Bridgeton **(U.S.-flag Commercial Tanker)**
    In July 1987 Iranians planted a mine that damaged the ship near Kuwait, 21-31, 36, 97-98

Brindel, Captain Glenn R., USN
    Served as commanding officer of the frigate *Stark* (FFG-31) when the ship was seriously damaged by Iraqi missiles in May 1987, 70-79, 92-93

Brink, Commander Dale D., USN
    In the late 1980s commanded the administrative support unit at Bahrain, 123, 129-131

Brooks, Rear Admiral Dennis M., USN (USNA, 1957)
    In 1987-88 commanded Joint Task Force Middle East, 47-50, 61, 63, 97-104

Brown & Root Corporation
    U.S. Navy use of the barges *WimBrown* and *Hercules* in 1978-88 as platforms for surveillance in the Persian Gulf, 37-51

Bull, Rear Admiral Lyle F., USN
    In 1987, as Commander Carrier Group Seven, was involved in planning for air support of Operation Earnest Will, 14-15, 113

Center for Naval Analyses
    In 1987 provided a representative to aid Commander Middle East Force during Operation Earnest Will, 52-54

Central Command, U.S.
    In the late 1980s was the unified commander for the Middle East, 2, 5-7
    Involvement in 1987 in the planning and execution of Operation Earnest Will, 10, 14, 97-100, 130-133
    CNO Carl Trost's view of the CentCom staff in the late 1980s, 130-133
    Headquarters at MacDill Air Force Base in Tampa, 132-133

Cobb, Commander William W. Jr., USN (USNA, 1968)
    In 1987 commanded the destroyer *Coontz* (DDG-40) during operations in the Persian Gulf, 68-69, 78, 92-93

Commercial Aircraft
    An Iranian airliner was shot down by the cruiser *Vincennes* (CG-49) in July 1988, 20-21, 82, 93

Commercial Ships
    In 1986 Iranians boarded the U.S. cargo ship *President Taylor*, 34
    In July 1987 Iranians planted a mine that damaged the tanker *Bridgeton* near Kuwait, 21-31, 36, 97-98

Iranians laid mines in 1987 in a commercial ship anchorage off Fujairah, United Arab Emirates, in the Gulf of Oman, 31-34

In October 1987 an Iranian Silkworm missile hit the tanker *Sea Isle City* in Kuwait, 53, 96-97

Congress, U.S.
Concerns in 1987 about the viability of conducting Operation Earnest Will in the Persian Gulf, 74

Convoys
Planning in 1987 for the escort of re-flagged Kuwaiti tankers during the Iran-Iraq tanker war, 11-19

Escort of tankers in the Persian Gulf in 1987-88, 15, 21-66, 86-100

In July 1987 Iranians planted a mine that damaged the tanker *Bridgeton* near Kuwait, 21-31, 36, 97-98

Iranians laid mines in 1987 in an anchorage off Fujairah, United Arab Emirates in the Gulf of Oman, 31-34

***Coontz*, USS (DDG-40)**
In May 1987 a U.S. Air Force E-3 Sentry tracked an Iraqi fighter headed toward the *Coontz* (DDG-40) in the Persian Gulf, 68-71, 76-78, 92-93

Crist, General George B., USMC
Served as Commander in Chief Central Command, 1985-88, 2, 5-7, 10, 29, 31-32, 38, 41, 44-47, 50-51, 60, 86, 113, 126, 131-132

Crowe, Admiral William J., Jr., USN (USNA, 1947)
Served as Commander Middle East Force in 1976-77, 16-17, 118

As Chairman of the Joint Chiefs of Staff in 1987 was heavily involved in the planning and execution of Operation Earnest Will in the Persian Gulf, 13-14, 16-19, 25, 44, 47-48, 51, 57-58, 113

Spoke at a news conference in July 1988 after the cruiser *Vincennes* (CG-49) shot down an Iranian airliner, 82

Damage Control
Performed by the crew of the frigate *Stark* (FFG-31) after the ship was hit by Iraqi missiles in May 1987, 73, 81-82

Desert Storm
Iraqi Mining of the amphibious assault ship *Tripoli* (LPH-10) in the Persian Gulf in January 1991, 48-49

Dittmer, David L.
Center for Naval Analyses representative who aided Commander Middle East Force in 1987, during Operation Earnest Will, 52-54

Dubai, United Arab Emirates
　Repaired damaged ships during the Iran-Iraq tanker war of the 1980s, 111-112
　In 1987, as military commander in Dubai, Sheikh Mohammed bin Rashid Al Maktoum agreed to U.S. overflights of the Musandam Peninsula, 113-118
　In the 1990s the Navy had problems with Dubai after a U.S. sailor killed a child with his automobile, 117-118

E-3 Sentry AWACS
　In May 1987 the U.S. Air Force plane tracked an Iraqi fighter headed toward the guided missile destroyer *Coontz* (DDG-40) in the Persian Gulf, 68
　In May 1987 a U.S. Air Force E-3 Sentry tracked an Iraqi fighter headed toward the guided missile frigate *Stark* (FFG-31) in the Persian Gulf, 71

Earnest Will, Operation
　Planning in 1987 for the escort of re-flagged Kuwaiti tankers during the Iran-Iraq tanker war, 11-19, 112-115
　Operation of the convoy escorts in 1987-88, 15, 21-66, 86-100
　In July 1987 Iranians planted a mine that damaged the tanker *Bridgeton* near Kuwait, 21-31, 36, 97-98
　Iranians laid mines in 1987 in an anchorage off Fujairah, United Arab Emirates in the Gulf of Oman, 31-34
　Use of the barges *WimBrown* and *Hercules* in 1978-88 as platforms for surveillance in the Persian Gulf, 37-51
　In October 1987 U.S. helicopters attacked Iranian Boghammars in the Persian Gulf, 48-50
　U.S. destruction of the Iranian Rostam oil platform complex in the Persian Gulf in October 1987 to retaliate for the *Sea Isle City* attack, 98-103
　Consideration in 1987 of the vulnerability of a battleship in the Persian Gulf, 105-107
　Use of AWACS during Operation Earnest Will in 1987-88, 109-110
　Logistic support of the operation, 39-40, 55-60, 119-130
　News media coverage of the Persian Gulf tanker war and Earnest Will in the late 1980s, 24-25, 66, 83-87

Exocet Missile
　French-made antiship weapon Iraqi planes fired at ships in the Persian Gulf in 1987, 68-69, 72

Fujairah, United Arab Emirates
　Site of an anchorage on the Gulf of Oman where Iranians laid mines in 1987, 31-34
　Served as a staging site for U.S. logistic support of Operation Earnest Will in 1987, 56-57

Great Britain
　In 1972 the British withdrew from East of Suez, including Bahrain, where the U.S. Navy took over the Juffair naval base, 119, 122-123

Opted not to get involved in the Iran-Iraq tanker war in the late 1980s, 8

Grieve, Captain David, USN
In the late 1980s served as ops officer on the staff of Commander Middle East Force during Operation Earnest Will, 19-20, 121

***Guadalcanal*, USS (LPH-7)**
Amphibious assault ship that entered the Persian Gulf in 1987 to support minesweeping helicopters, 30, 34

Gunnery-Naval
U.S. destruction of the Iranian Rostam oil platform complex in the Persian Gulf in October 1987 to retaliate for the *Sea Isle City* attack, 98-103

Guns
Installation of 25-millimeter guns in U.S. Navy ships involved in Operation Earnest Will in 1987-88, 51-52

H-53 Sea Stallion
Helicopters used for minesweeping in the Persian Gulf in 1987-88, 30

Habitability
On board ships of the Middle East Force in the Persian Gulf in the late 1980s, 88-89

Helicopters
Support of Operation Earnest Will in the Persian Gulf in 1987-88, 13, 19-20, 30, 35, 37-40, 48-49, 51, 72, 123

***Hercules* (Oil Platform Service Barge)**
Used as a base for U.S. surveillance of the Persian Gulf in 1987-88 during Operation Earnest Will, 37-51

Howard, J. Daniel
In the late 1980s served as Assistant Secretary of Defense for Public Affairs, 83-84

Hoyt, Captain Michael C., Supply Corps, USN
In 1987-88 provided direction to the logistic support efforts in Bahrain for Operation Earnest Will, 128-129

Hussein, Saddam
Iraqi dictator whose agents gassed Kurds in 1988, 93-95
His 1990 invasion of Kuwait led to Desert Shield/Desert Storm, 62

Intelligence
The United States had limited information on Iranian decision-making in the late 1980s, 24

U.S. intelligence in connection with Operation Earnest Will in 1987-88, 31-33, 97-98

Investigations
Rear Admiral U.S. Grant led the investigation of the damage to the frigate *Stark* (FFG-31) when she was hit by Iraqi missiles in May 1987, 74-78

***Iowa* (BB-61)-Class Battleships**
Consideration in 1987 of the vulnerability of a battleship in the Persian Gulf, 105-107

Iran
Friendly relationship with the United States in the mid-1970s, 17
In the mid-1980s Iranian aircraft were shot down by the Saudis over the Persian Gulf, 42-43
Engaged in an anti-tanker war against Iraq in the late 1980s, 1-2, 7-12, 17, 35-36, 67-68, 94-95, 112
In July 1987 Iranians planted a mine that damaged the tanker *Bridgeton* near Kuwait, 21-31, 36, 97-98
Iranians laid mines in 1987 in an anchorage off Fujairah, United Arab Emirates in the Gulf of Oman, 31-34
In September 1987, U.S. forces captured the Iranian minelayer *Iran Ajr* in the Persian Gulf, 19-20
In October 1987 U.S. helicopters attacked Iranian Boghammars in the Persian Gulf, 48-50
In October 1987 an Iranian Silkworm missile hit the tanker *Sea Isle City* in Kuwait, 53, 96-97
U.S. destruction of the Iranian Rostam oil platform complex in the Persian Gulf in October 1987 to retaliate for the *Sea Isle City* attack, 98-103
U.S. air and surface attacks on Iranian warships during Operation Praying Mantis n the Persian Gulf in April 1988, 22-23, 116-117
Iranian political leadership in the late 1980s, 21-24
An Iranian airliner was shot down by the cruiser *Vincennes* (CG-49) in July 1988, 20-21, 93
The Iran-Contra Affair in the late 1980s was not helpful to Commander Middle East Force, 85-86, 93-95
Operation Southern Watch, U.S. air surveillance of Iraq from 1991 to 2003, 110-111

***Iran Ajr* (Iranian Minelayer)**
Captured by U.S. forces in the Persian Gulf in 1987, 19-20

Iraq
Engaged in an anti-tanker war against Iran in the late 1980s, 1-2, 7-12, 17, 22, 68, 94-95, 112
Use of French fighter planes to attack ships in the Persian Gulf in 1987, 22, 68-69, 71-74

An Iraqi pilot attacked the guided missile frigate *Stark* (FFG-31) on 17 May 1987 in the Persian Gulf and caused significant material damage, 67, 71-74, 79-81, 92-93

In the wake of the *Stark* incident, the U.S. and Iraqi forces developed deconfliction procedures to facilitate communications, 91-92

Iraqi mining of the amphibious assault ship *Tripoli* (LPH-10) in the Persian Gulf in January 1991, 48-49

Isa ibn Salman Al Khalifa, Sheikh

As Emir of Bahrain in the 1980s and 1990s had a personal relationship with Bernsen, 118-122

***Jarrett*, USS (FFG-33)**

Participation in Operation Earnest Will in the Persian Gulf in 1987, 19-20

Jesberg, Rear Admiral Ronald H., USN (USNA, 1959)

In the late 1980s served as Commander Naval Forces Central Command, 52, 128-129

Joint Task Force Middle East

Established in September 1987 to command Operation Earnest Will in the Persian Gulf, 47-50, 97-104

***Kidd*, USS (DDG-993)**

Destroyer that escorted convoys in the Persian Gulf as part of Operation Earnest Will in 1987, 27-28

Kuwait

In 1986-87 appealed to other nations for protection during the Iran-Iraq tanker war, 7-10

Planning in 1987 for the operation of Kuwaiti tankers under the U.S. flag to facilitate escort by the U.S. Navy, 11-19

From 1987 to 1990 the Kuwaitis provided fuel to the U.S. Navy, 13, 57-66

Execution of the convoy escorts in Operation Earnest Will in 1987-88, 15, 21-28

In July 1987 Iranians planted a mine that damaged the tanker *Bridgeton* near Kuwait, 21-31, 36, 97-98

In October 1987 an Iranian Silkworm missile hit the tanker *Sea Isle City* in Kuwait, 53, 96-97

Kuwaiti Oil Tanker Company

Involved in 1987-88 in the escort of its tankers after they were transferred to the U.S. flag, 12, 29, 39-41, 58, 61

***La Salle*, USS (AGF-3)**

In the mid- and late 1980s served as flagship for Commander Middle East Force, 3-5, 67-72, 74, 84, 87, 98

In port on 17 May 1987 when the frigate *Stark* (FFG-31) was severely damaged by Iraqi-launched Exocet missiles, 67-72

Site of the 1987 investigation into the damage to the *Stark*, 74

Less, Rear Admiral Anthony A., USN
Commanded the Middle East Force in 1988, 20, 22, 116-117

Logistics
Support of Operation Earnest Will in the Persian Gulf in 1987-88, 54-66
From 1987 to 1990 the Kuwaitis provided fuel to the U.S. Navy, 13, 57-66

***Long Beach*, USS (CGN-9)**
In the autumn of 1987 was the flagship for Rear Admiral Dennis Brooks, Commander Joint Task Force Middle East, 99

Lugo, Captain Frank J., USN
In 1987 was a special projects officer on the staff of Commander Middle East Force, 41, 45-47

MacDill Air Force Base, Tampa, Florida
Site of the headquarters of the U.S. Central Command, 132-133

Mail
Distribution of in 1987-88 to units of the Middle East Force, 123, 129-133

Middle East Force, U.S.
Buildup of the staff in 1987 and increase in number of ships as the result of the Iran-Iraq tanker war, 3-4
Planning in 1987 for the operation of Kuwaiti tankers under the U.S. flag to facilitate escort by the U.S. Navy, 11-19
Execution of the convoy escorts in Operation Earnest Will in 1987-88, 15, 21-66, 86-100
In 1987 the staff got outside help by representatives for the Naval Science Advisory Program and the Center for Naval Analyses, 52-54
In 1987-88 Commander Middle East Force did not see the need for Aegis cruisers in the Persian Gulf, 107-109

Military Sealift Command
In the late 1980s its tankers picked up free oil from Kuwait to support Operation Earnest Will, 59-64

Mine Warfare
In July 1987 Iranians planted a mine that damaged the tanker *Bridgeton* near Kuwait, 21-31, 36, 97-98

Iranians laid mines in 1987 in an anchorage off Fujairah, United Arab Emirates, in the Gulf of Oman where, 31-34

U.S. minesweeping assets in the Persian Gulf and Gulf of Oman in 1987-88, 29-30, 34, 36-37

In September 1987, U.S. forces captured the Iranian minelayer *Iran Ajr* in the Persian Gulf, 19-20

The frigate *Samuel B. Roberts* (FFG-58) was damaged by hitting an Iranian mine in the Persian Gulf in April 1988, 27-28, 48-49, 116-117

Iraqi mining of the amphibious assault ship *Tripoli* (LPH-10) in the Persian Gulf in January 1991, 48-49

Mirage F-1 Fighter
Iraqi plane that fired Exocet missiles at ships in the Persian Gulf in 1987, 68-69, 71

Missiles
Iran's use of during the tanker war in the Persian Gulf in the late 1980s, 23, 48, 53, 96-97

Iraq's use of during the tanker war in the Persian Gulf in the late 1980s, 68, 71

The cruiser *Vincennes*, USS (CG-49) shot down an Iranian airliner in July 1988, 20-21, 93

Mohammed bin Rashid Al Maktoum, Sheikh
In 1987, as military commander in Dubai, agreed to U.S. tactical flights over the Musandam Peninsula for "humanitarian" missions, 113-118

Naval Reserve, U.S.
Officers from the Naval Control of Shipping organization served as liaison to merchant ships during convoy escorts in the Persian Gulf in 1987-88, 15-16

Naval Science Advisory Program
In 1987 provided a representative to aid Commander Middle East Force during Operation Earnest Will, 52-54

News Media
Coverage of the heavy damage to the frigate *Stark* (FFG-31) in May 1987, 79-83

Coverage of the Persian Gulf tanker war and Operation Earnest Will in the late 1980s, 24-25, 66, 83-87

News conference at the cruiser *Vincennes* (CG-49) shot down an Iranian airliner in 1988, 82

Nimble Archer, Operation
U.S. destruction of the Iranian Rostam oil platform complex in the Persian Gulf in October 1987 to retaliate for the *Sea Isle City* attack, 98-103

***O'Bannon*, USS (DD-987)**
In early 1987 served as temporary flagship for Commander Middle East Force, 5

Oil
    Iran-Iraq tanker war in the Persian Gulf in the late 1980s, 1-2, 7-14
    From 1987 to 1990 the Kuwaitis provided fuel to the U.S. Navy, 13, 57-66
    Planning and execution of Operation Earnest Will in 1987-88, 11-66, 86-100

Persian Gulf
    Site of Iran-Iraq tanker war in the late 1980s, 1-2, 7-9
    In the late 1980s served as home base for the Middle East Force flagship *La Salle* (AGF-3), 4
    Planning in 1987 for the operation of Kuwaiti tankers under the U.S. flag to facilitate escort by the U.S. Navy, 11-19, 112-118
    Execution of the convoy escorting in 1987-88, 15, 21-66, 86-100
    In July 1987 Iranians planted a mine that damaged the tanker *Bridgeton* near Kuwait, 21-31, 36, 97-98
    Iranians laid mines in 1987 in an anchorage off Fujairah, United Arab Emirates, in the Gulf of Oman, 31-32
    U.S. Navy use of the barges *WimBrown* and *Hercules* in 1978-88 as platforms for surveillance in the Persian Gulf, 37-51
    U.S. destruction of the Iranian Rostam oil platform complex in the Persian Gulf in October 1987 to retaliate for the *Sea Isle City* attack, 98-103
    Consideration in 1987 of the vulnerability of a battleship in the Persian Gulf, 105-107
    In 1987-88 Commander Middle East Force did not see the need for Aegis cruisers in the Persian Gulf, 107-109
    Iraqi Mining of the amphibious assault ship *Tripoli* (LPH-10) in the Persian Gulf in January 1991, 48-49
    Effect of the climate and weather on U.S. ships operating in the Gulf in the late 1980s, 87-89

Planning
    Planning in 1987 for the operation of Kuwaiti tankers under the U.S. flag to facilitate escort by the U.S. Navy, 11-19, 112-118

Powers, Captain Robert C., USN (USNA, 1960)
    Consideration in 1987 of the vulnerability of a battleship in the Persian Gulf, 105-107

Praying Mantis, Operation
    Air and surface attacks on Iranian warships in the Persian Gulf in April 1988, 22-23, 116

Quainton, Anthony C. E.
    Served as U.S. Ambassador to Kuwait from 1984 to 1987, during Operation Earnest Will, 8, 12-13

Radar
In 1987 was used by U.S. ships and aircraft to detect planes flying in the Persian Gulf, 69-70, 78
Effect of climate on shipboard radars of the Middle East Force in the Persian Gulf in the late 1980s, 88-89
In 1987-88 Commander Middle East Force did not see the need for Aegis cruisers and SPY-1 radar in the Persian Gulf, 107-109

Rafsanjani, Akbar Hashemi
Chairman of the Iranian Parliament and de facto commander in chief of the armed forces from 1980 to 1989, 21-23

Rapid Deployment Joint Task Force, U.S.
Relationship with Commander Middle East Force in the early 1980s, 6

Reagan, President Ronald W.
Involvement indirectly with Operation Earnest Will in the late 1980s, 89-90, 103

Rogers, Rear Admiral David N., USN (USNA, 1959)
In 1987 negotiated deconfliction procedures for communication between U.S. and Iraqi forces, 91-92

Rules of Engagement
Application of by U.S. forces in and near the Persian Gulf in 1987-88, 19-21, 25-26, 34-35, 49-50, 70-71, 89-91, 98
British warships in the Persian Gulf in 1987-88 operated under more restrictive rules than did U.S. ships, 90

Samuel B. Roberts, USS (FFG-58)
Frigate damaged by hitting an Iranian mine in the Persian Gulf in April 1988, 27-28, 48-49

Saudi Arabia
In the mid-1980s shot down Iranian aircraft over the Persian Gulf, 42-43
In 1986-87 did not feel sufficiently threatened by the Iran-Iraq tanker war to provide basing rights to U.S. tactical aircraft, 11
Use of as a base for AWACS aircraft during Operation Earnest Will in 1987-88, 109-111

Sea Isle City (U.S.-flag Commercial Tanker)
Hit by Iranian Silkworm missile in October 1987, 53, 96-97

SEALs
Involvement in Operation Earnest Will in the Persian Gulf in 1987-88, 41, 46-47, 99

Sharp, Rear Admiral Grant A., USN (USNA, 1960)
Led the investigation of the damage to the frigate *Stark* (FFG-31) when she was hit by Iraqi missiles in May 1987, 74-78

Silkworm Missile
Iran's use of during the tanker war in the Persian Gulf in the late 1980s, 23, 53, 96-97

Southern Watch, Operation
U.S. air surveillance of Iraq from 1991 to 2003, 110-111

Soviet Navy
Increased presence in the Persian Gulf during the Iran-Iraq tanker war in the late 1980s, 9-10

Soviet Union
Relationship with Kuwait during the Iran-Iraq tanker war in the late 1980s, 7-10
As a possible threat to the United States in 1987-88, 16

***Stark*, USS (FFG-31)**
Pre-mission briefing for threat on northern station in the Persian Gulf, 70-71
Frigate that was attacked by Iraqi-launched missiles on 17 May 1987 in the Persian Gulf and suffered crew fatalities and significant material damage, 67, 71-73, 89-93
Follow-on activities, including damage control and investigation, 70, 73-78, 81-82
Transport of the bodies of the dead crew members to the United States, 79
News media coverage of the damage to the ship and loss of crew members, 70-83

***Tripoli*, USS (LPH-10)**
Damaged by an Iraqi mine in the Persian Gulf in January 1991, 48-49

Trost, Admiral Carlisle A. H., USN (USNA, 1953)
In 1987, as Chief of Naval Operations, visited the Persian Gulf during Operation Earnest Will, 61, 64-65, 129-133

United Arab Emirates
Iranians laid mines in 1987 in a commercial ship anchorage off Fujairah, United Arab Emirates in the Gulf of Oman, 31-34
In the late 1980s took a neutral stance in the Iran-Iraq tanker war, 111-113
In 1987 Sheikh Mohammed okayed U.S. tactical aircraft flights over the Musandam Peninsula for "humanitarian" missions, 111-118
In the 1990s the Navy had problems with Dubai after a U.S. sailor killed a child with his automobile, 117-118

***Vincennes*, USS (CG-49)**
Shot down an Iranian airliner in July 1988, 20-21, 82, 93

Walker, Rear Admiral Edward K. Jr., Supply Corps, USN (USNA, 1954)
   In 1987 provided personnel to help with logistic support of Operation Earnest Will in the Persian Gulf, 55-57, 128, 133

Weather
   Effect of the climate and weather on U.S. ships operating in the Persian Gulf in the late 1980s, 87-89

WimBrown **(Oil Platform Service Barge)**
   Used as a base for U.S. surveillance of the Persian Gulf in 1987-88 during Operation Earnest Will, 37-51

Zakhem, Sam
   In the late 1980s served as U.S. Ambassador to Bahrain, 56, 68, 124

Zeigler, Commander Howell Conway, USN
   In 1987-88 was the intelligence officer on the staff of Commander Middle East Force, 32-33

www.ingramcontent.com/pod-product-compliance
Lightning Source LLC
Chambersburg PA
CBHW080612170426
43209CB00007B/1408